# A Flying Fighter

**VINTAGE AVIATION LIBRARY**

*Night Raiders of the Air* by A. R. Kingsford

*Wings of War: A German Airman's Diary of the Last Year of the Great War* by Rudolph Stark

*A Flying Fighter: An American Above the Lines in France* by Lieut. E. M. Roberts

*The Flying Flea: How to Build and Fly It* by Henri Mignet

*French Warbirds* by 'Vigilant' (Claud W. Sykes)

*Flying Fury: Five Years in the Royal Flying Corps* by James McCudden, VC

*Over the Balkans and South Russia, 1917–1919* by H. A. Jones, M.C.

*An Airman's Outings with the RFC* by Alan Bott

*Green Balls: The Adventures of a Night Bomber* by Paul Bewsher

*Zeppelin Adventures* by Rolf Marben

*In The Royal Naval Air Service* by Harold Rosher

*A German Airman Remembers* by Hans Schröder

*Fighter Pilot* by 'McScotch'

*Jagdstaffel 356* by M. E. Kähnert

*Death in the Air: The War Diary and Photographs of a Flying Corps Pilot* by Wesley D. Archer

*Aces and Kings* by L. W. Sutherland

*etc., etc.*

# A Flying Fighter

**An American Above the Lines in France**

## Lieut. E. M. Roberts, R.F.C.

**GREENHILL**

This edition of *A Flying Fighter:
An American Above the Lines in France*
first published 1988 by Greenhill Books,
Lionel Leventhal Limited, Park House,
1 Russell Gardens, London NW11 9NN

This edition © Lionel Leventhal Limited, 1988

All rights reserved. No part of this publication may be
reproduced, stored in a retrieval system or transmitted
in any form by any means electrical, mechanical or
otherwise without first seeking the written permission
of the Publisher.

British Library Cataloguing in Publication Data
Roberts, E. M.
A Flying Fighter: An American Above the Lines in France
(Vintage Aviation Library 19)
1. World War I. Air Operations by Great Britain.
Royal Air Force – Biographies
I. Title  II. Series  940.4′4941′0924

ISBN 1-85367-006-5 Hardcover
ISBN 0-947898-98-0 Paperback

Publishing History
*A Flying Figher* was first published in 1918 (Harper & Brothers)
and the text is reproduced exactly as the original edition,
complete and unabridged.

The Publishers are pleased to acknowledge the kind assistance
of the Library of the RAF Museum, Hendon, in making
this edition possible.

**Greenhill Books**
welcome readers' suggestions for books that might be added to
this Series. Please write to us if there are titles which
you would like to recommend.

Printed by Antony Rowe Limited,
Chippenham, Wiltshire.

# CONTENTS

| CHAPTER | | PAGE |
|---|---|---|
| I | A Start at Soldiering | 1 |
| II | Getting Near the Front | 16 |
| III | Gassed | 26 |
| IV | Sped by Machine Guns | 36 |
| V | Running the Gauntlet | 47 |
| VI | Wounded Again | 65 |
| VII | Joining the Flying Corps | 80 |
| VIII | My First Flight | 97 |
| IX | My First Hun | 112 |
| X | My Commission | 124 |
| XI | Battering the Hun | 138 |
| XII | "Pizz" and "Randie" | 147 |
| XIII | Daredevils | 162 |
| XIV | The Big Push | 175 |
| XV | Learning to Fly | 201 |
| XVI | Stunts and Accidents | 226 |
| XVII | Air Battles over the Lines | 245 |
| XVIII | Back to Blighty | 267 |
| XIX | Old Times and New | 287 |
| XX | Meeting the King | 299 |
| XXI | In the Clouds | 320 |

## APPENDIX

Just Flying Man's Talk . . . . . . . 333

To
THE MEMORY OF
CAPTAIN E. A. BURNEY
Killed in action on the Somme
July, 1916

## PUBLISHER'S NOTE

ALTHOUGH Lieutenant Roberts's modest preface makes little reference to the exploits which he has lived through, the readers of the extraordinary story which follows may care to know a few personal facts at the outset. It was in 1914 that this adventurous young American enlisted, and it was early in 1915 that he reached the Western Front. It was not until November, 1917, that he returned to this country. In that time he won his commission and more than won the air-fighter's title of Ace, for in his battles he has brought down not merely five but seven Huns. His victories did not leave him unscathed. He was wounded four times in midair, once at the Battle of the Somme. And certainly after such service there is a story to tell which, as it seems to those who have known it, has not been equaled in its own field for intensely human interest and dramatic quality.

New York, 1918.

## PREFACE

THIS is the story of three years of active service on the Western Front, most of the time in the Flying Corps. I hope that the story will interest readers. If not, it certainly will not be the fault of my experiences in themselves.

The leaders of the Allied forces in Europe have realized long since that air service is one of the premier branches of the military establishment. The aerial observer has come to be the eyes of the army. It is he who often brings the first news that the enemy is getting ready for an offensive. Upon him the commanders rely for information as to all movements behind the enemy lines. The aerial observer directs the fire of his artillery, and, finally, when the men go over the top, he is often the sole means of communication between headquarters and the firing line.

It is needless to say that the enemy is not

## THE FLYING FIGHTER

in ignorance of the great service rendered by the airman. To cripple that service as much as possible he sends up his own aviators, especially when his anti-aircraft batteries have failed him. It is then that the man aloft is called upon to defend himself as well as those on the ground, to whom he is giving the best that is in him. Then comes the aerial duel. And in most cases one of the combatants crashes to the ground—it has been his last flight.

These are the things which I have set down here.

But I have not overlooked the humorous side of the airman's life. After nerve-racking hours in the air the necessity for relaxation is great, and then he generally applies himself to that with the same vigor that marks his conduct while on duty. Ours is a short life, so why not make the most of it while it lasts? That is the axiom of all birdmen.

But while there are plenty of thrills in this fighting in the air, I have not written solely for the purpose of entertainment. My three years at the Front have made me realize

## PREFACE

more than ever that the Great War is not yet won. It has been said a thousand times that this is not simply a War between armies. Since my return from the battleground I have asked myself the question: To what extent does the American public realize that the World War is a titanic struggle between all the economic resources and forces of the nations involved rather than simply a war between the fighting armies?

I have come to the conclusion that Americans generally do not recognize this in spite of the introduction of meatless and wheatless days and coal saving. The reason seems to be that we are too far away. We are handicapped by distance. So far the United States has only begun to feel the War, as its effects are measured in European countries. Let us hope that realization of the War's meaning and responsibilities will become general before it is forced home by hundreds of thousands of casualties. Efficient preparation will prevent losses in the end.

E. M. R.

New York, February, 1918.

*For I dipt into the future, far as human eye could see,*
*Saw the Vision of the world, and all the wonder that would be;*
*Saw the heavens fill with commerce, argosies of magic sails,*
*Pilots of the purple twilight, dropping down with costly bales;*
*Heard the heavens fill with shouting, and there rained a ghastly dew*
*From the nation's airy navies grappling in the central blue;*
*Far along the world-wide whisper of the south wind rushing warm,*
*With the standards of the peoples plunging thro' the thunder-storm;*
*Till the war-drum throbb'd no longer, and the battle-flags were furled,*
*In the Parliament of man, the Federation of the world.*
—From "Locksley Hall," *by* ALFRED TENNYSON.

# CHAPTER I

### A START AT SOLDIERING

An American, born in the city of Duluth, Minnesota, I had inherited a love of adventure which asserted itself strongly while I was young. When a lad ten years old, I ran away from home and started out to see the Great Northwest and make my own way in the world. And since that time the greater part of my schooling has been in the University of Hard Knocks. A great many of my companions were men made famous by Jack London in his works; indeed, Jack himself was a good friend of mine, having done me many a good turn; in fact, he once saved my life.

After leaving home, I was attracted by the woods and took up lumbering. But after an accident in a sawmill, I had to give it up.

## THE FLYING FIGHTER

Then I crossed the border over into Canada and from that time on I took up anything and everything. I went into mining, then I went into the automobile game. Then I tried railroad construction work, cow-punching, sheep-raising, and when war broke out I was up in the foothills of the Rockies drilling for oil. It will seem incredible when I say that the Battle of the Marne and the first battle of Ypres were matters of history before I knew that there was a war, and that the greater part of the civilized world was arrayed against Germany and German Militarism. In October, 1914, I started from the plains for a short visit to Calgary. On my way I had to catch a train at Okotokos, where I had bought a steak which was wrapped up in a newspaper. Butchers and customers in that country were not particular in matters of hygiene. I saved the paper to read, for I had been away from all settlements for some weeks and had heard nothing of the War. The headlines broke the news to me that Germany had taken it upon herself to decide the questions of the day by the sword. It struck me that this would provide the excitement I had

## A START AT SOLDIERING

been looking for. But I little thought when I first saw those headlines that from that time on my fate would be in the hands of destiny and that the breaking of log jams on the Five Miles Rapids in the Mississippi, service with the Sheriff's posse chasing cattle thieves, and shootups in the barrooms of cow towns where half the participants were killed would all be like pink teas compared with what lay before me on the Western Front of the Great War.

I had come to Okotokos for the purpose of having a couple of days in which to clear up some freight which lay in the yards. In spite of that, I soon found myself on the way to Calgary, where I figured on having a few days with friends whom I had not seen in a long time. I had come ninety miles from my camp, making the trip in a day and a half in my eagerness to see town.

At Calgary I met an old friend of mine called Ross, but known to his intimates as "The Fish," from the fact that he was a native of Nova Scotia. We shook hands and sailed a few schooners across the bar of the good hostelry where I had put up. The only thing we talked of was the War. "The Fish" told me there had been a call that morning for some two or three hundred men for service in Europe, and he added, "Let's join." I said, "Jake," meaning all right, as that was exactly what I expected to hear from Fish, for I knew him to be an adventurer and a good fellow. And though neither of us had ever soldiered a day in his life, we made up our minds to join the forces that were being raised if they would have us. We spent the greater part of that night talking war and killing a few regiments of Huns over the cup that cheers.

Next morning the papers were full of what the Germans were doing in Belgium and that increased our determination to enlist. We were a little cautious, however, and before starting for the recruiting place we looked up a friend and had him explain to us the formalities that would have to be gone through. The only advice he could give was that if we didn't hurry up, it might be all over before we enlisted. This was quite enough and inside of two hours I was a member of the Tenth Canadian Infantry Battalion.

## A START AT SOLDIERING

After taking a look at the barracks I thought it no more than prudent to straighten out my personal affairs. My boss, an American by the name of Saunders, thought I was crazy and said so.

"Before you get over there, the war will be over," he said.

"And before it is over you will get into it," I returned.

I cannot recall now whether I meant that or not, but, as the saying goes, many a true word is spoken in jest. Ten months later, Mr. Saunders had taken up recruiting work for the Canadian Government, being too old for service in France.

As a parting present he gave me a box of cigars, together with the good advice one generally hands out to a young man about to become a soldier.

I returned to the barracks and did my best to find military life agreeable. While the call issued had been for three hundred men, at the most, about seven hundred actually volunteered, so that I thought myself lucky to have been accepted.

The officer in charge of the barracks knew

me quite well. He also knew of my familiarity with mechanics, and for that reason caused me to be transferred to a mechanical transport section. I cannot say that this pleased me greatly. That job seemed a little too tame. At any rate I thought that my days in the zone of danger were over then and there. Later, however, I was to find out that this was a very premature conclusion, especially when trench warfare, and warfare of several other kinds, came to be my daily lot.

I managed to get my pal, "The Fish," transferred with me, and that helped both of us to get over the rude shock to which our great enthusiasm had been subjected. The day after enlisting we were sent in a western draft column to Valcartier, Quebec. Henceforth, "fours right" and "fours left" got to be all there was in life.

"Evoluting" on the camp ground gave me a new opinion of military life. I could not see why on earth we had to do all this when they wanted men in France. Of course, I had a hazy notion that discipline was necessary, and that I should not call the Colonel "George" on parade. But why all this walk-

## A START AT SOLDIERING

ing? My idea of warfare was to fight from tree to tree and rock to rock in the manner which once was famous in the West. I knew nothing of trenches and cannot say that I cared to know anything about them. My vision of handling shovels was too closely associated with railroad building and mining. I have done pick and shovel work in my time and it seems to be an excellent occupation for men with weak minds and strong backs. But not for me.

However, they have the knack of shattering dreams around military camps. Mine went with the rest, but the cause, for which I had enlisted, seemed so good that I resolved to put into practice the meaning of the motto —Everything is worth trying once. Moreover, soldiering did not seem so very uninteresting, despite its routine and restrictions. Finally, here was the chance of seeing a new country.

Weeks and weeks of training were our lot. It was a case of getting up at 5:30 in the morning in temperatures that seemed to stay more or less around 30 degrees below zero. After getting up we would run several times around a race track for exercise, have breakfast, and then spend the greater part of the day in similar body and mind hardening work. I will confess that had I known what was in store for me no team of horses could have dragged me into an army. My idea had been that I should be given a uniform and a gun; then I would sit down and wait for orders to sail to France and get into the thick of it. Some of the boys grumbled a little at the delay, but in the end we all made up our minds that now we were in it there was nothing to do but stick to it and hope for the best. The first seven years would be the worst, said some kind people, intending to be facetious.

But all things come to an end, and so did the eternal setting-up drills at the camp. Finally I got a job driving one of the heavy motor trucks, known in the British Army as a "lorry." Not very long after that I was made a sergeant in a mechanical transport section and sent to Toronto, Ontario, to train with the Second Division.

This transfer was not what I had been looking for. I had hoped to stay in the

## A START AT SOLDIERING

mobile army and get some fighting in the line. But people had a knack of remembering that I knew a little about the automobile, and in Canada such men were rare.

The order came that all Americans were to be ousted from the army. But the Commanding Officer called the Americans together and asked us if we wanted to take our discharge or not. One man did this but the rest of us stayed. We were required to sign new attestation papers, but before we could do that, we had to select some particular part of Canada as our nominal birth place. I stated that I was born in Sasalta, Alberta. Another man said that he hailed from Toronto—in fact, none of us had any trouble finding fictitious places of birth in the Dominion until it came to Tom Kelly, of Chicago, who had given the matter no thought. To the officer who questioned him, he said that he was born in Beansville. The officer wanted to know where Beansville was located, and Kelly replied:

"Oh, somewhere in Fish Country."

The officer promptly put down Beansville, Nova Scotia, and everything was in order.

## THE FLYING FIGHTER

I didn't drive the lorry very long after that, being set to work to initiate recruits into "fours right and left," "sections and half-sections," and the like. When not occupied with drill I would take a turn as orderly (dog) sergeant of the day, mount guard at night, and see that everything was clean and ship-shape in the little zone that was mine, in order to please the officer of the day when he did his rounds.

There was also a great deal of clerical work to do. I had to write all the passes for the men getting leave to go into town. With that came responsibilities, which often were irksome. The passes for the men had to be taken to the Commanding Officer for his consent and signature, and when the officer refused to honor one of them, I generally was blamed for it, especially when a fellow had made an appointment with some young lady.

There was a fence around the camp and many a man, refused admission to go to town, had his first experience there at "going over the top." And though the top of the fence was lined with barbed wire, the boys put a

## A START AT SOLDIERING

plank over it, and many a night that plank worked overtime. To get back into barracks was a little more difficult, however; but generally the man who had gone without leave straightened things out with one of the guards, and so avoided trouble with the authorities.

Intoxicating drinks of any sort were prohibited in camp, but for all that many a bottle was smuggled in, even after systematic search of the men returning from town. Some of the men were most resourceful in finding places where they could hide the flasks. They would secrete them in their riding breeches, in their caps, and when this no longer worked, they went so far as to buy cakes a little larger than a flask, hollow them out and then put the bottle in it. These delicacies were supposed to come from home and the guards were fooled for a long time until one day a cake made a most peculiar noise as it was being examined by a non-commissioned officer. As he shook the cake, a familiar sound fell upon his ears. It sounded like liquor in a bottle. Whereupon this avenue of importing intoxicants into the camp was closed, and the sergeant inspector was richer by one bottle, which was divided among the guard.

It was an easy thing in those days to get kicked out of the army altogether, for men were still plentiful, and one had to be almost a physical marvel to get into the service at all.

We spent some time in a camp on the shores of Lake Ontario, where uniforms were finally issued to us. The funny little coats they gave us, and the regulation breeches had a queer look about them; I felt that my friends back home, had they seen me in this get-up, would have had me examined as to my sanity. For riding breeches were only used by the idle rich, in the Northwest.

The underwear they issued us was even more of a trial. It was rough and a person putting it on for the first time had the impression that the "kooties" had settled all over him, as indeed they did in the case of many.

Though I had done everything possible to keep these insects away from me, I discovered that my efforts were unavailing. It got to be a question of how to get rid of the pests,

## A START AT SOLDIERING

and, having heard of a method that would accomplish this, I thought that I would try it. We had a dog for a mascot, and dogs, as everyone knows, have fleas. It is said that there is eternal enmity between kooties and fleas and that one will not stay where the other is. With that in mind, I transplanted a few of the fleas upon myself, so that they might declare war upon the kooties and drive them out. But before the experiment could be successfully concluded, I thought it well to apply a chemical remedy; anyway the desired result was obtained, which gave me what I hoped for.

By this time most of us had become familiar with the little tricks of barrack life. We had a good doctor, who thought nothing of excusing us from drill and other hard work so long as we said that we were sick. The result of this was that many of us were sick every cold morning that came along, especially when the night before we had done overtime playing poker and rolling the "bones."

The money that was won at these games was in I. O. U.'s generally, but now and then one actually managed to get some real cash. Gambling got to be a mania with us and the gang would sooner play poker than eat. It ultimately reached a point where the men would play for everything and anything, even their shoes. And the Doc got wise, and after that when a man went sick he got a dose of castor oil at the very least.

Our military training was making some headway, however. We came to understand the different bugle calls, and we learned how to handle the rifle and bayonet and how to shoot.

We were now told that our training would be completed in England; France seemed as far away as ever. Most of us thought that the war would surely end before we got there. As week after week passed away the chances of seeing the battlefield seemed more remote.

But one fine day in March we received orders to get ready to entrain. There was much hustle and happiness—faces were glowing, and the old grudges were forgotten. The preparations for our departure were made in jig time. A few telephone calls to wives,

## A START AT SOLDIERING

mothers and sweethearts, and the men were ready.

On the day of our departure the camp grounds were packed with relatives and friends who came to say good-bye; in the case of many it was to be a last farewell.

# CHAPTER II

### GETTING NEAR THE FRONT

NEEDLESS to say, we had a hearty reception everywhere on our trip East. Within six hours of our arrival at Halifax the organization had embarked and was on its way to Europe.

The first thing that attracted my attention on our arrival in Liverpool was the funny little English trains. The coaches with their compartments did not impress me favorably, but I found them quite comfortable for all that. They were so packed that some of us had to sit on the floor. I also discovered that these little English trains could move at a mighty good speed.

At about one o'clock in the morning we stopped, detrained, and made a long march to the camp which had been made ready for us. There we were given blankets and a cup of

## GETTING NEAR THE FRONT

hot tea; and then we turned in and soon everybody was fast asleep, the railroad trip and the march having made us a weary crew, indeed. Next morning, at reveille, we found that we had come to England for no other purpose than to continue the dull drilling that we had left off in Canada. This was disappointing, but we were set to work to get over it. It had been raining and the mud was deep enough to lose your shoes in. We were not used to wet weather and within two or three days the sick parade was bigger than usual, and not a few of us were laid up for a long time. The climate proved too much for me also. Chills had settled all over me, and I was hoarse, but despite that I continued my duties. On one occasion I was in charge of the sick parade and as I marched the men over to the doctor I had practically no voice left. The doctor had some difficulty in understanding me, but he was quite cheerful about it.

"What's the matter with you this morning?" he inquired. "You make a sound like a codfish."

I explained that I did not know exactly what

was the trouble, so the doctor took my temperature and called the ambulance. I was to be taken to a hospital, the very thought of which gave me the shivers. I suggested to the doctor that possibly the affair could be settled without going to the hospital.

"Well," he said, "if you don't go now your friends will be walking slowly behind you next week."

That seemed good advice to me, especially since I was under the spell of the big medical term which the doctor had made use of so casually—bronchial pneumonia.

I managed to survive the attack and upon return to my unit found that the Commanding Officer had decided to give me back pay and three days' leave to go to London, a city which I then saw for the first time.

The British capital was known to me only through a few pictures of the more important places, such as Westminster Abbey, the Tower, and St. Paul's Cathedral. But I had heard a lot about Leicester Square, Hyde Park, the Strand, Charing Cross and Piccadilly Circus, and I wanted to see them. As a natural result, at two o'clock in the morn-

## GETTING NEAR THE FRONT

ing, after my arrival, I found myself lost in the streets of London. I stated my trouble to a very obliging Bobby, who was somewhat handicapped in helping me, for the reason that I had forgotten the name of the hotel where I was stopping. There was nothing to do after that but to hire a taxi and spin around until I should have located the place, some hazy notion as to its locality being still in my mind. The taxi hadn't gone more than thirty yards when I saw the house for which I had been looking so anxiously just across the street. And there I learned that the London taxi driver knew his business, and also how to charge.

But further adventures were to come. A day or two after my arrival in town I thought I would like to see Piccadilly Circus, hoping, of course, to find a big tent and a lot of side shows, and all that goes with an establishment of the sort. I asked a Bobby for directions and I remember his making the remark:

"This 'bus goes right through it."

Thinking that the omnibus was a "Circus Special," I started on my ride without bothering much about my destination. There ought to be no trouble finding out when I was at the circus. After a ride of about half an hour the conductor climbed up the stairs for another fare.

"Say, isn't it near time we got to Piccadilly Circus?" I said.

"Why, you went through there about twenty minutes ago," he replied. "You are out at Clapham Commons now."

There was no doubt that I had missed the Circus, but I was still anxious to see it and started out once more in quest of it. I took another omnibus, gave the conductor his four pence, climbed on top and rode until I felt sure we must be somewhere near the Circus. Just then the conductor came up for another fare. I wanted to know where Piccadilly Circus was.

"Why, man, this is Hyde Park Corner," he replied. "We went through the Circus about five minutes ago."

Having fifteen minutes the best of the first lap, there was nothing to do but get off that 'bus and think it over for a while. It seemed a little strange that I should be constantly

## GETTING NEAR THE FRONT

going through the Circus and not see anything of it. I decided to try a taxi, to the driver of which I gave particular instructions to take me to Piccadilly Circus and drop me off in the middle of it. The man smiled and drove off. In about three minutes he stopped and opened the door for me to get out. I looked around for a circus but saw none. The only thing that came at all near reminding me of a show were some flower girls near a fountain. Under the circumstances it seemed best to take the taxi driver into my confidence. After much explanation on my part, which afforded not a little amusement to the chauffeur, I learned that Piccadilly Circus is a sort of semi-circular place into which lead seven thoroughfares from the several parts of the city.

The constant traveling I had done on the 'buses had given me a very good appetite, and to appease it I walked into the first place I came to. This happened to be one of London's ultra-fashionable tea parlors. The place was fairly well packed at the time but I managed to find a place at a table. I noticed that everybody was sipping tea and eating cakes, but that was not the sort of food I was looking for. The waiter wanted to know whether I had come to take tea, to which I replied that a steak about the size of a barn door, done rare, and served with fried onions, would suit me much better. The man's jaw dropped and everyone around began to smile. I was informed that this was a tea-room and not a restaurant. Too timid to leave the place, I ordered some tea and ate about two dollars worth of biscuits before I had satisfied my appetite. I found out then and there that the cost of living in England was higher than I had thought. It was just as well that my stay in London was limited to three days.

Upon my return to the camp I found that I had been transferred to a mechanical base to drive a mobile workshop. This detail gave me a good opportunity to see much of rural England and its beautiful scenery. The fine old trees especially interested me, as did the lovely old-fashioned houses, the fine lawns and well-kept orchards; also the hop fields.

A little later I was one of those picked to go to France in a draft for the mechanical

## GETTING NEAR THE FRONT

service. Little by little I was moving up closer to the front. There was a possibility of running into a submarine or "tin fish," as the Boys called them, while crossing the English Channel, though it was known that they were not out in full force just then. We landed in France after an entirely uneventful journey, and in a little French *estaminet* we drank our first French wine. It did not taste good to me; in fact it was sour. I noticed, however, that there were many good-looking girls about the place and they made a much better impression upon me than the wine had done.

On the same afternoon I made the acquaintance of the French railroads, the passenger cars of which are just as funny and little as those of the English lines. We traveled in freight cars, however, which are large enough to carry, as stated by a signboard on the sides of the car, forty men or eight horses—40 *hommes ou 8 chevaux.*

In this manner we got to a railroad where we were met by an English sergeant-major and taken to a camp which was about six miles behind the lines.

## THE FLYING FIGHTER

We thought that we were real soldiers now. The Commanding Officer of the base to which we had been taken was not of that opinion, though. The sergeant-major, who had been our reception committee, had brought us to attention before the Commanding Officer with results that did not seem to have pleased either of them. The Commanding Officer gave us to understand that we were to be drilled and have discipline instilled into us even if he had to do it with a sledge hammer. That was definite enough, but we had the satisfaction of knowing that we would not stay in that place forever, consequently we let his remarks go in by one ear and out by another.

There was a businesslike air about the place which impressed us all the more when presently they issued to each of us a rifle and fifty rounds of ammunition, and assigned us the lorries we were to drive.

Before the day had grown much older I was given a good lesson in discipline. There was a queer mark on the body of the lorries —a triangle with a bar in its center. I wanted to know what that meant, but was given to understand that it was none of my "blink-

## GETTING NEAR THE FRONT

ing" business. All I had to do was to drive that lorry and keep it clean. There was a great deal of terseness about that remark, and I decided not to ask any more questions that seemed out of order.

Before long that old wagon became to me bedroom, sitting-room and what-not, all rolled into one. It wasn't such an uncomortable home at that.

My lorry belonged to a column that carried ammunition from the nearest railhead to the front. The first hurry call we had lasted three days. The Huns were getting busy on the salient. On arriving at the advance dump —the place where the gun-limbers get the ammunition for the batteries—I heard shells scream for the first time in my life. It gave me a peculiar sensation at first, though some-one said cheerfully:

"Oh, you'll get used to this."

For all that, I always retained a wholesome respect for a high explosive shell.

# CHAPTER III

### GASSED

On the morning of the first day of the second battle of Ypres, I happened to be doing some repair work on the section commander's automobile. In a nearby field was an artillery ammunition dump, and this the Germans seemed bent upon reaching with their shells. The fire was scattered, however, and before long it became entirely too hot around the car I was repairing and I was obliged to find shelter in a bomb-proof. There was a lull in the fire presently, and I concluded that it might be safe to resume my work. I had hardly come to the surface, however, when the Huns reopened their fire. It seemed best to get in the car and speed as far away from the front as was possible. I had gone down the road some two hundred yards when the section commander caught up with me and demanded his car, saying that he was in a

## GASSED

hurry. So I jumped out and let him have it.

The fire continued and I could not see what good it would serve to stay in it. While I was walking along the road, about three-quarters of a mile behind the lines, the firing increased in intensity. The noise fascinated me. For about two hours I watched the spectacle of a front in eruption.

There was heavy firing all night, and the next morning I suddenly smelt something like chloride of lime. The stench increased all the time, and presently my lungs began to feel sore. I had a hard time breathing, and coming to a ditch I looked into it to see whether the smell was coming from there, chloride of lime being used generally for sanitary purposes. But I saw nothing in the ditch and my lungs began to hurt more and more. Finally I took my bandanna handkerchief and tied it over my mouth. A few minutes later an ammunition lorry came tearing down the road. It picked me up and took me to the railhead, where, with four others, I was sent to a hospital and treated for gas poisoning. In three days I was sent to England with about twelve hundred other men who had been gassed or wounded.

That was only one ship-load, however. Several thousands of other wounded and gassed men followed us. Many of them were Canadians whose organizations had lost heavily in the second battle of Ypres, for it was the first time gas had been used on the Canadians. They were a heart-breaking sight, and I thanked my stars that I still had a whole skin.

The effects of the gas poisoning were not so easily gotten rid of, however. The cure was painful. It consisted for the major part of taking a lot of salt water and other emetics so that the system might be cleared of the gases assimilated by the lungs. The lungs remained congested for quite some time, and a peculiar irritation in the throat caused me on several occasions to cough myself into insensibility.

The gas patient is a hard case for the hospitals. I got very little sleep, mainly for the reason that I was tied up in bed in a sitting position, which, in the course of time, made me very ill-tempered and caused me to use

## GASSED

language which afterward I regretted. Also I discovered that the hospital was under martial law, and that this law was enforced as rigorously here as anywhere else. That helped me to settle down and take things as they came, but there were times when I thought very seriously that it would be better to die.

One day a doctor came to the hospital and picked out two patients he wished to cure at home. I was one of them. The other man had been wounded in sixteen places and was a terrible sight. When I saw him first it was believed that he would die, but within a few days he recovered sufficiently to stand the transfer from the hospital to a place called Hawkhurst, near the doctor's home in Kent.

The two of us were given a large front room. But I could not stand the sight of my companion in misery. So he was presently taken to another part of the house. I can't remember the name of the man, but I know that he belonged to the artillery and that a Hun shell had burst about a foot above his head. His scalp was terribly lacerated and a piece of shrapnel had entered at the side

## THE FLYING FIGHTER

of the nose and emerged at the side of the neck. One of his eyes was black and closed, and the other eye he seemed unable to ever close. The only part of his body that was not bandaged was his right forearm, and that moved day and night.

I think he was conscious part of the time, for now and then he would utter a loud groan that made me jump. Fearing that the man was dying, I would call the night nurse and she would summon the doctor, a man who had the patience of Job, as was shown one night when he was called six times and still managed to be pleasant and cheerful. He really deserved a medal for his unfailing good temper.

The people in that part of the country were very anxious to make us as comfortable as possible, and they even got permission to take me to their homes. One old gentleman, of the name of Hardcastle, took me all over his place. He was somewhat of an American, having operated at one time a cattle ranch in New Mexico.

Of course the odor I had mistaken for the smell of chloride of lime was that of German

## GASSED

chlorine gas. I had breathed only a little of it and the effect had been bad enough. The troops on the firing line had suffered terrible losses from the gas. Shortly after that gas masks were issued and though they were very inconvenient, they were indeed life-savers and we welcomed them.

After my discharge from the hospital I was attached to a mechanical transport column in England and in August, 1915, we received orders to proceed to France. The trip to the nearest seaport had to be made over the country roads. I was section sergeant and in this capacity had to scout the roads ahead of the column, on a motor cycle, thereby gaining the title of "The Human Sign Post." In addition to that I had to keep the convoy together. We passed through a lot of little English towns and lived mostly on bully beef and hard tack, though occasionally the farmers and villagers along the road would ask us to eat with them.

Trouble seems to come in bunches, and I had several such bunches on that trip. As section sergeant I was riding a motor cycle, usually at great speed, with the result that my face was all wind-burned. The men, moreover, seemed bent on raising Cain before getting to France. There are a good many parallel roads in the parts of England we were going through, and often there are no signs on them. Since some of the fellows did not like the big clouds of dust that were being raised by the motor trucks in front, they would hang back and take some other road, usually the wrong one. That kept me busy. Keeping the convoy together at night, when often I had trouble with the headlight of the motor cycle, which had gone on strike, was no easy work. The roads all had high trees on each side, which made them look very much alike and kept them all the darker at night.

Hunting stray motor trucks under these conditions was not easy and generally so many were missing that I had to keep racing back and forth at high speed. One night I was hurrying along one of these roads, steering by a speck of sky visible under the tree crowns. Suddenly I came to a turn in the road, missed it in the dark and ran full speed into a high hedge. The motor cycle landed

## GASSED

in the ditch and I was catapulted over the hedge in a somersault. I had just come to a sitting position when somebody spoke to me. It was the colonel of an artillery camp who was on his rounds of inspection. He found my sudden arrival in his camp very funny, and laughed over it. Then he helped me back over the hedge. I found that the machine was still in working order and decided to take time to fix the headlight. Fortunately, I was none the worse off for the fall.

The convoy made good progress, however. Accidents were few. The most serious of them happened one day while we were going through a little village. One of the lorries hit a milk cart in the stern and drove the horse through a store window. But nobody was hurt. Another few miles brought us to our goal—the seaport—though before we actually reached it I hit a cement block about a foot high while going at the rate of thirty miles an hour and had a very fine spill.

It did not take us long to embark the convoy and a few days later we arrived at Rewan, in France, where we spent two days resting up. Then the convoy was formed into column and started for the front.

We were required to travel as fast as we could, stopping only for our meals of bully beef and hard tack. For three weeks that was the only thing we had to eat, and upon our arrival at the first parking place, we began working day and night, to gather up and feed the Second Division, which was just then pouring into France ready to get into action.

Some of the machines were detailed to pick up stragglers, who were dropping out of the ranks during the long route marches over cobble-stone roads, while others were engaged in filling up the railhead with provisions and forage. This sort of thing continued until we got closer to the advanced railhead, and there our real work began.

But before we got that far, two others and myself who had motor cycles made a trip to the nearest first line trenches where we had some friends. To do that was not easy, but we had no real trouble until we got to where the road pickets were. These we bluffed with the usual statement that we had dispatches. I may say that we did not always get away with the bluff. Some of the road pickets would want to see our identification papers as dispatch riders, and being unable to produce the goods we were often turned back. In that case we would ride a short distance down the road, get off our cycles, cover them with leaves and branches so that no one could see them, and then crawl around the picket on hands and knees until we were out of sight.

We were all right as soon as we got to the communication trenches, so long as we knew the name of the battalion we wanted to visit. Many queer things happened on these side trips. A pal of mine, named Emory, was caught in the wrong sector and though he had proof of his identity, the Commanding Officer, to teach him a lesson, made him go out into No Man's Land to a listening post. After having been thoroughly scared by the Huns and reprimanded by the Commanding Officer of the battalion, Emory was sent back to his unit.

# CHAPTER IV

### SPED BY MACHINE GUNS

LITTLE excursions to the firing line were the only diversion the men of the column had. They also gave us a chance to see a little more of war than running a lorry allowed. I had friend in nearly all of the battalions, and among my pals in the infantry was a fellow named Brown, who came from the Pacific Coast. I used to supply him with cigarettes and the like.

On one of the windy and rainy afternoons they get in the autumn in Flanders, I had gotten through a little earlier with my work and decided to see Brownie, for whom I had bought some socks. I managed to get past the road sentries all right and entered a little town called D. B. The place has long since been razed. On the other side of the little town there is a shallow lake about a mile and a half wide, which I would have to

## SPED BY MACHINE GUNS

wade in order to reach my friend. Going through that lake was not an easy matter. While one could be guided by the blasted tree stumps, along the submerged road, the ground had to be carefully inspected with one's feet if the many shell holes in the road were to be avoided.

Going along the road this afternoon I fell into three shell craters and had to swim to get out of them, which was not an easy job on account of the clothing I had on. I managed to get to the other side of the lake, but found that only a few of the communication trenches were safe. Though I was none too pleased with my trip by now, I decided to go on. To keep under cover I made up my mind to go through a little woods, on the other side of which the British lines were located. I had a disagreeable experience among the trees. I stepped on a grave and the odor that came out of it was sickening.

It had grown dark. I hung my coat on the cross at the head of the grave and lit a match to read the name on it—Private Bolton, Black Watch, the number of his regiment and the date of the action in which he was killed.

## THE FLYING FIGHTER

Before the match died out I could see that there were more of these crosses and from inquiry I learned that some nine hundred Black Watch and Scots Greys were buried there. I was also told that the continual rains were gradually washing away the earth of the graves and thus exposing the dead.

My informant was a sniper and he and I talked war until a working party came up. It was going the same way I was and I decided to go along. We had to cross an open spot about fifty yards in width, and the Huns, who were on the side of a slope about a hundred yards away, knew it. Working parties and others going to the first line trenches also had to cross the exposed field. Every fifteen or twenty minutes the Germans sent up flares or star shells to light up the approach to the trenches. Whatever they saw was sure to be machine-gunned. Many a poor chap went down on that lonely and barren spot.

The locality was dismal in the extreme. On the few trees that were standing hardly a branch was left. The ground was mucky despite the efforts that had been made to regu-

## SPED BY MACHINE GUNS

late the rain water by means of sand bags. It seemed to me that in Flanders they have nothing but rain. It came drizzling down in a world that was all gray except when lighted up by the star shells of the Germans, which would throw a ghostly light on the surrounding country and then make it look all the more lonesome. I only wished that I were back in North America.

I did not like the idea of going over the exposed field and decided to cross it by means of an old French trench I had noticed. But I had not gone very far in the trench when I found it was closed with sand bags to keep out the water that was coming from the other side, so that a part of the trench might be used as shelter against the German machine-gun fire.

There was nothing to do but to get out of that trench again, but before I did that I picked up some French cartridges which I wanted to keep as a souvenir. In doing that I discovered that dead men had been buried in the trench but had evidently been uncovered by the rain. There was nothing to do but go to the front line with the working party which was just starting across the exposed spot one at a time. The men would start as fast as legs could carry them. Spurred by the thought that the German machine guns might hit them they traveled *some*.

The Boche had learned, however, that the working party was on its way across, and as each man started to run the machine guns would speed him on his way.

The machine guns worked with a rapidity of six hundred shots a minute. The fourth man of the working party was half way across the open field when he pitched head first to the ground and lay still. The next man rushed to where the other had fallen, picked him up, swung him on his back, and then continued his running as fast as he could.

The star shells of the Germans came closer together now, and the machine guns fairly rattled at the two men.

We stood there with open mouths, hoping that the man carrying the wounded would not get hit and in our hearts we cursed the Huns who were doing the shooting.

## SPED BY MACHINE GUNS

The man finally gained a trench on the other side of the open ground, much to our relief. At least one of the men was safe.

The race with death started anew. Other members of the working party rushed across the open space as fast as they could. One of them fell, but he rose again and continued his mad race for the trench opening beyond.

It got to be my turn. A rubber coat I was wearing hampered my movements and also reflected much of the light of the star shell which just then went up. I was nearly in the middle of the exposed field when Fritz started his machine gun and caused me to move faster than before. My speed was a surprise even to me, and, despite the fact that I was hampered by the weight of wet clothing, I approached the opening of the trench on the other side with such momentum that I was carried past it; I landed head over heels in a telegrapher's dugout and knocked his stew and fire all over the shack.

I had deprived that man of his supper after he had risked his life to get some wood across the open space. He was drawing for his fuel supplies on a shell-blasted house about two hundred yards behind our line.

The man cursed me roundly, for which I do not blame him. He had been flirting with death to get enough wood for his supper and now I had spoiled it all. For two weeks he had lived on bully beef and hard tack.

I squared myself by giving him a pocket alcohol lamp which I always carried with me. That appeased his wrath, and he was kind enough even to direct me to the first line trenches.

To get to the first line of the trenches I would have to take a certain communication trench, said the telegrapher. I started off through the deep mud, entered at the opening of the communication trench, but found that the ditch had been plugged up with sand bags to keep the water out.

It was the practice during rainy weather to cut off sections of the communication trenches in order that they might remain passable. The rain water collected in the deeper lying parts, from which it was lifted by means of hand pumps.

To get out of the communication trench at

the "plug" meant to run once more into the machine-gun fire of the Germans. But there was no help for that. So I went over the top and reached the next stretch of the communication trench on the double quick. After a seemingly interminable wade through the mud, which formed the bottom of the trench, I finally got into the British first line to find that my pal was on picket. It would be an hour before I could see him.

That time I spent in the company commander's dugout watching through the periscope the star shells of the Germans. It was a splendid free fire-works show.

Brownie showed up finely and appreciated both the cigarettes and the socks I had brought him.

I hadn't seen my friend in quite some time and there were many things we had to tell one another—in whispers, of course, because we were only a few yards away from the Hun trenches.

Of a sudden some machine guns near us began to pump lead. Peeping over the parapet of the trench we saw that the British had taken under fire an ammunition party of the

## THE FLYING FIGHTER

Germans, which just then became visible through a gap in a stone fence. It seems that the Hun ammunition carriers had been observed a little further away. But they were in the habit of using the fence as cover. They would be fired upon promptly every time they reached the gap. The British were now sending up star shells so constantly that the countryside was lit up almost as well as if it had been day. The machine guns kept up a lively racket and presently they were joined by the rifles of the men in the trenches. The field artillery also took a hand in the affair and before long a very lively scrimmage was going on. They seemed to have plenty of ammunition just then. It was either that or the probability that somebody had mistaken the nature of the fight, which caused the howitzers and the heavier pieces also to be heard from. For over an hour the slam-banging continued and since there was no telling what the thing might develop into, I wished Brownie good-bye with a promise that I would see him again soon.

On my way back I fell from one mud hole into another and generally had a very good

## SPED BY MACHINE GUNS

taste of what soldiering at night means. Walking in the mud was the hardest of work. It was a case of pulling your foot out of twelve inches of muck, sticking it in again and then repeating the operation. By the time I got to the dugout of the telegrapher I was dead tired. The thought occurred to me that I would ask the man to let me stay with him for the night, but I feared that he was still angry over the loss of his stew.

There was nothing to do but go on. I managed to cross the open field without being shot at and so got into the little woods. On the edge of the lake I fell into a smokebox hole. In my struggle to get out of it I exhausted myself so that I had to lie down in the mud and rest up a while. Then I waded through the lake, weighing a ton by this time, so it seemed. My clothing was wet, I was tired out, and the mud also added to my burden.

I was thankful when I got back on the main road where the mud was less sticky and not so deep. It was three o'clock in the morning before I got into camp, and at five o'clock I was on the road again with my convoy to fetch material for the Royal Engineers, to whom I was then attached.

I had not had a chance to take off my clothing. When I looked myself over in daylight I saw that I was mud from head to foot and that there were six bullet holes in my raincoat. The bullets must have gone through the coat while I was running across the open ground with the coat standing out straight behind me owing to the speed I was making. The boys found my adventure of the night quite interesting, and I bet some of them two weeks' pay that I could outrun them under any circumstances.

# CHAPTER V

### RUNNING THE GAUNTLET

Our work at that time consisted principally of carrying barbed wire to the front through mud and slush of which there seemed no end. Northern France and Flanders seemed to be all mud in the winter—perhaps in summer too.

A few nights later the section commander ordered me to make up a convoy of seven three-ton trucks and proceed to H—— for twenty tons of coal. The drivers of the unit were men from all over the world. I had a Canadian, an American, an Australian, an Englishman, a Scotchman, a Swede, a Welshman, and a Frenchman. They were all men who had lived well in civilian life and the eternal stew of bully beef, and the hard tack, made for them a very monotonous bill of fare. The motor truck drivers anyway never lost a chance of getting better grub than the army ration, so at the railhead, where the French were unloading a merchandise train, some of my men looked around for something to eat. We found only six tons of coal, which we loaded on two of the lorries, and while the men were doing that I went to the base commander's office to find out about the rest. While I was away from the unit the idle men looked over the French army supplies, and soon found that they could use some of them. They helped themselves to a lot of canned goods. The prospects of getting a square meal were too tempting to be overlooked. The trouble was that the boys were not satisfied with little; instead of taking a few cans they took several cases, and when I came back a French officer had my men lined up and a couple of gendarmes were going through the lorries looking for the stolen goods.

I was not surprised for I knew my ever-hungry horde too well to think that they would overlook such a chance to get something to eat. But for the sake of appearances I asked some of the men if there was anything wrong. The French officer told me that they were being searched for stolen

## RUNNING THE GAUNTLET

goods. That settled it, for I knew that they had been found out, otherwise the French officer would not have gone so far as he did. There was a fine chance for all of us being placed under arrest and courtmartialed. I thought the thing over quickly, went over to one of the lorries, pulled the gendarme out of it, and then shouted at the other. I asked them who had given them permission to search my lorries and was told that the French officer had ordered it. There was nothing else to do now but try issues with the officer. I went over to him and asked him by what authority he was searching British lorries without my consent or the consent of the British base commander. That was walking on thin ice, of course. The base commander was an Englishman and I was a colonial; I doubt very much if he would have given me protection. I asked the French officer for his name and address, and told him that I would report him to my commanding officer. That helped. My strategem succeeded, and rather than have more fuss the French officer thought it best to call off the gendarmes. And on returning to camp I was

## THE FLYING FIGHTER

given an invitation to a canned chicken dinner by my men. Of course, I knew where it came from.

I was coming down the road one night with a load of barbed wire and pickets when I noticed a man who had a flash lantern in his hand. I did not know what the man wanted and stopped the lorry. When I got down in the road I noticed that he was dressed in an officer's uniform and saluted him. He wanted to know where we were bound for. The officer wished to go in the same direction and asked me to take him along, which I did. When we had started again he told me that he was the commanding officer of a Canadian pioneer battalion. I had been under the impression that I knew the man, but had been unable to recall who he was. Finally, I thought I had him placed, but was still not altogether sure. At any rate I told him that I had seen him before; just then I remembered that the last time we had met it had cost me $30. The officer looked at me in surprise as I mentioned this interesting fact, and I inquired whether he was not Magistrate Saunders of Calgary, Alberta. He said that

## RUNNING THE GAUNTLET

he had filled such a position at one time and that his name was Saunders. Then I told him who I was and I reminded him how on a certain occasion he had not allowed me to say anything for myself but had just tacked on the $30 fine for exceeding the speed limit with a motor car. We had a good laugh and parted the best of friends.

Hauling material at night for the Engineers in a neighboring sector, we had to use a road on which several dispatch riders had been killed by a spy. It had been announced that two weeks' leave of absence in England would be given the man who caught the spy, and of course everybody was on the lookout for him. Every nook and cranny in that part of the country had been searched, but nobody had been found. The only person ever seen near the road was a peasant plowing his fields.

About a week after that I met a sergeant of the police whom I knew well and he asked me to come with him next morning to headquarters. I was there at six o'clock and at six-thirty that same peasant was marched out in the little square behind the chateau and

## THE FLYING FIGHTER

blindfolded. Sentence of death was then read to him and for the first time in my life I saw a firing squad march out. It was over soon. A bullet through the heart put an end to the peasant and he was buried without ceremony as a traitor to France and the Allies.

The sight impressed me greatly and for the first time I realized fully what it meant to be a traitor. I went back to the ammunition dump a very thoughtful man, realizing how little a life mattered in this great struggle.

That afternoon, the weather being for once favorable, both sides sent up their captive balloons. I counted as many as twenty of them. Most of them were Germans. We had a few ourselves, but the Germans were better equipped in that respect. The aeroplanes also sailed about.

I envied the flyers. Here was I in mud up to my knees either in the trenches or on the roads and getting very little out of the war but lots of hard work. The other fellows were sailing around in the clean air while I had to duck shells all the time and run chances of being caught by the machine guns

## RUNNING THE GAUNTLET

and snipers. Of course the aviators were also being shelled, but they never seemed to get hurt. I had seen some of them hit trees and other obstacles upon landing or getting off the ground, but the game had always appealed to me strongly. To me flying seemed the very acme of adventure and I had no notion, of course, how good the German anti-aircraft batteries were. Flying "fish-hooks," burning "onions," as we term a certain type of shell used by the Hun, and forced landings were things unknown to me. Of the cold above the clouds and the chances one took in having to land behind the German lines I had heard very little.

But I was willing to take a chance for all that, so long as I could get out of the mud and had an opportunity to stay indoors at night. The mechanical transport service was famous for mud and night work. I was so thoroughly sick of them both that I was willing to do anything to get away from them.

During the next few days I tried to gather information as to how I could get into the Royal Flying Corps. I got no satisfaction, however, for nobody seemed to know exactly how so exclusive a circle could be invaded. Nevertheless, my ambition to get into the aviation service grew stronger each day, and each bit of information I could secure was welcome.

Christmas of 1915 came around, and every man at the front was looking forward to it on account of the presents and better food from home which the holiday season would bring. The officers of the unit were to give us a turkey dinner. The day before Christmas we were paraded and each man received a pair of socks, a piece of good maple sugar, and three packs of cigarettes. From some other source we received a deck of cards and a small box of chocolate. Many of the boys also received Christmas boxes from home, but I was not one of them.

On the same afternoon I witnessed an event that to me really seemed worth while. Some Canadians were to be decorated by the French for deeds of valor. We were away north of the French lines, but that made no difference to the poilus, who also were to attend the ceremony. They came down in lorries just as they had left the trenches and

## RUNNING THE GAUNTLET

they did not have a holiday appearance. There were about five hundred of them.

After the French soldiers had been lined up with bayonets fixed, the men to be decorated, twenty-eight in number, were marched into the square that had been formed. This done, some of our own troops marched up, headed by a band that was playing the Marseillaise. The enthusiasm was great. Those men had gone through every hardship one can imagine, and to see some of their comrades honored seemed to cheer them all. The poilus and our own men were not exactly a clean looking lot. There was an unwashed look about their be-whiskered faces and on the mud-covered gray coats could be seen many a blood-spot. But the men were as steady as rocks and presented arms with a snap that was really inspiring.

As the British forces came to attention the French band struck up the "Maple Leaf Forever," and followed this by "Old Canada." Then the French and British generals shook hands, and later the French general pinned the decorations on the Canadians and kissed each of them on the cheek, while our kilted band played the march past. When it was all over the generals again saluted each other and the troops dispersed. The men who had been decorated did not seem to know what to do with themselves. Just then the gang who had watched it all rushed upon the poor unfortunates and carried them shoulder high to the nearest café.

It had been a most impressive affair. There is something in those French soldiers and even in the peasants that make one conscious of the fact that the French are indeed a noble race. They were already beginning to feel the great strain of the war, and though they showed plainly that it was telling on them, they were bearing up wonderfully. I used to ask them whether they were anxious for peace; always they said yes, but with the terms of ourselves and our allies—the terms of the victors. Otherwise they were willing to fight to the last and I think they have shown that spirit all the way through.

Christmas evening we had the turkey dinner. Those who were in the front lines had theirs the next day. The front was quiet. At twelve o'clock on Christmas eve all

## RUNNING THE GAUNTLET

firing had ceased and only an occasional star shell reminded us that night that war was still on. These shells are sent up to guard against surprise attack. We wished one another all the good things of the season and we even included the Huns, who were about seventy-five yards away. They had hoisted up a placard over the parapet on which was inscribed the words Merry Christmas. It was a sight that touched the hearts of many of us and one that we will not forget in a hurry.

We were a rather melancholy crew those days. Everybody's thought seemed to be very far from the trenches.

Somebody would shout:

"Hey, mate, what are you thinking about?" and back would come the answer:

"Aw, shut up!"

Many of us would have given a great deal to be home that night, especially when at one o'clock in the morning the Christmas truce came to an end with the bark of the rifles and the tut-tut-tut-tut of the machine guns. Soon the field artillery and the "heavies" woke up again, and before long an intense bombardment of the sector was on. When daylight came the ambulances were busy carrying out the wounded and dying and many were buried on Christmas Day.

That afternoon I received two letters from home and two others from friends in England, which was really a big mail. I also received a very small box about the size of a jewelers' case and very neatly done up. I was curious to know what it contained, and upon opening it found Turkish cigarettes—lady size, or about the dimensions of a wooden match. They had been sent me by a lady with whom I had had tea in England and who had promised to send me cigarettes. I sat down and finished the lot, all of them making just one good smoke. I ended the day with a visit to a dugout where we had a game of poker, in which I won twelve dollars, which was a lot of money, seeing that our pay was only a franc, or twenty cents a day.

This meant that I had in my pockets a fair percentage of the company's pay-roll. I knew that I would have to loan out a considerable share of it before long and that very little of it would ever be paid back.

## RUNNING THE GAUNTLET

With some of my winnings I managed to secure a bath, something which is pretty hard to get in Flanders, since the natives do not seem to bathe very often. In Flanders the bath is taken in a wooden tub in the kitchen, and one has to scout around until some peasant woman is found who is willing to rent her kitchen for that purpose. Taking a bath is quite an event in that part of Europe. I was once billeted in a peasant woman's house where nobody had taken a bath for seven months. The woman had the habit of washing the children's faces in the same water in which she had washed the dishes. After that I took no chance on her cooking, and a partner of mine, Will Askey, and I took turns attending to our food.

During our first months in France we had near us a Gurka or Indian regiment. And it was funny to see the little brown men in camp or in action. They were very interesting. The Gurkas eat a funny cake made by themselves of flour and water and you could walk into a Gurka camp most any time and see some of them squatting in a circle making their funny little biscuits of flour and water which, when cooked, had no taste whatever.

They also drank a lot of coffee of the French kind, which is about seventy-five per cent chickory and twenty-five per cent coffee, but it isn't bad to drink at that.

The Huns had a wholesome fear of these little Gurkas, for they are wicked fighters, and they used to call them the "little black devils." The Gurkas, when ordered over the top, climbed over the parapet, dropped their rifles and pulled out their "kukries," a sort of heavy knife which is curved and looks for all the world like a hand-scythe for cutting corn.

This knife was carried in their mouths by the Gurkas, who, crawling up to the Hun lines on their stomachs, would bounce into the Hun trenches and without a word the silent slaughter would start. They would cut a Hun's throat, then cut off his ears as a keepsake, and one can imagine the terror the Hun must have experienced when he saw those wicked little beady eyes full of murder looking at him.

When the Gurkas returned, they would take

## RUNNING THE GAUNTLET

their German ears, dry them and string them around their necks as our old North American Indians hung scalp locks around their belts. And if a Gurka had to go to a hospital, you could take his clothes or anything else he had, but you could not touch the string of Hun ears he wore around his neck. All the Canadians liked the Gurkas very much, for they were excellent fighters, and we all hated to see them taken away to another and warmer front where the climate was more suitable for them, and where it was easier to procure certain kinds of food which they could not get along without.

I was still hoping that sooner or later I might get into the Royal Flying Corps, but the chances did not seem very good. I was still living in the mud and working chiefly at night for the reason that during the day German artillery made all roads of approach to the position impossible. Neither the mud nor the night work looked good to me, but for the time being there seemed to be no getting away from them.

One night about six o'clock I received orders to report at an engineer's dump known

## THE FLYING FIGHTER

as Hyde Park Corner. I was to bring two lorries which were to be loaded with barbed wire and steel pickets. At the dump I was told to proceed to R. E. Farm, the road to which took us through a shell-torn village. On entering the village we had to leave the main road because that lay in full view of the enemy. At the other side of the village the road was re-entered at a point where there was a screen of sacking, on one side of which were painted in large letters the words: "Danger! In full view of the enemy!"

About fifty feet from the screen an old woman used to keep a coffee wagon from which she sold refreshments to working parties who used to wait behind the screen until dark made it possible for them to get to the front.

This particular night Fritz had a hunch that somebody was going to pass the place behind the screen. Just as I was approaching the coffee wagon the Huns began to send over shells and the third one landed right underneath the wagon and blew it, the lady, and the old horse into Kingdom Come.

## RUNNING THE GAUNTLET

It was bad enough to have the old lady and the horse killed, but to lose that coffee stall and that *café complêt* was really the worst of all. *Café complêt* in this instance meant that a liberal shot of rum went into each cup of coffee.

We would have to do without that now, and the thought exasperated us. Fritz had been guilty of an unforgivable sin, as anyone would have concluded from the language that was used by the boys. In the meantime the shells were still coming and it seemed extremely risky to continue on the road, which was so narrow that only one truck at a time could pass over it. There was a side road, but that had three feet of mud on it, nor were we inclined to run back three-quarters of a mile to get another road. The sentry near the screen let us pass, but I knew that the lorries would have to get up better speed if they were to cross the danger zone unhurt.

By means of a governor, the speed of the lorries was being limited to fifteen miles an hour. But we had discovered that if the ball in the governor was held up we could get as much as twenty-five miles out of the motor.

# THE FLYING FIGHTER

I was heading the column and knew that if my lorry went faster the others would know what to do, so I climbed in front of the machine, lifted the hood and held up the ball in the governor. It did my heart good to see the speed the motor was giving the car now. The other drivers followed my example and before long we were tearing down the road with the shells falling all about us. We had gone another mile and a half towards the dump, when a small shell hit one of the armored front wheels of my lorry and blew it off. The lorry fell on its axle, but aside from being strained a little and having lost a wheel it suffered no damage. We managed to get a spare wheel and by midnight were on our way back to the camp.

# CHAPTER VI

### WOUNDED AGAIN

FIVE days later I had a like experience while carrying lumber to the front for the repair of a field dressing station about two hundred yards behind our lines. To get there exposed ground had to be traversed. There was a similar screen of sacking at that point, and the sentry who directed the traffic on the road did not want to let me pass. To lend force to his arguments he drew my attention to a nearby field, in which, though only about three hundred yards square, there were as many as 150 shell holes. As I was counting the holes, a heavy bang nearby showed me that some of our forces were stationed there, and then I knew why the Germans had dug up the field so well. They had been looking for this battery for some time and that accounted for the many shell craters.

I waited at the screen until it was nearly

dark and then continued. My lorry had been seen, however. As I was taking it around a corner the Huns cut loose and caused me to go down that road as fast as the motor would take me. I had climbed through the head of the lorry and was lifting up the hood to release the governor, when I received so forceful a punch in the hips that I was almost knocked off. We did not stop but went right on and upon arrival at the dressing station, about two miles from the point where I had been hit, the doctor picked a bullet out of my side. Fortunately, it was a spent bullet and aside from having the wound sterilized I needed little attention. In a few days I was back at work.

On that trip also I saw a mule hit on the head by a shell, which showed me what annihilation really meant, as it blew its head off.

Shortly after my return from the hospital Sergeant Arthur Montgomery Dyas and I started for the ruins of Ypres in the Canadian salient to get some furniture for a sergeant's mess. We got to the place without any trouble and found cover for the lorry in the lee of a blown-up building. It was a fine day and a

## WOUNDED AGAIN

Hun *Taube* was sailing overhead. The British anti-aircraft batteries were concentrating upon the airplane, with the result that a great deal of shrapnel began to fall around us. We had to get under cover, but anxious to see what would happen to Heinie aloft, we ventured out again. The British batteries were getting the bead on the *Taube*. In the blue sky around the aircraft shrapnel clouds were visible and gradually came closer to the machine. Of a sudden the flash of a shrapnel appeared directly under the machine, which seemed to come to a stop immediately, then broke in two and came hurtling to the ground. It hit the earth with a crashing sound.

I was still very much interested in military aviation, but for a moment I wondered whether, after all, that game was worth while.

The German batteries began to look for revenge and very soon the battery that had brought down the Hun birdman received their close attention. The ruins of the town were not overlooked. Masonry, bricks and the fragments of shells filled the air, but the only casualty I noticed was a large rat that had made up its mind to cross the road. A piece of a shell hit the rat. It died then and there. Montgomery looked at me and I looked at him, and I guess both of us had the same thought: even a rat hadn't a chance in those parts.

After a while the bombardment ended, and then we started to hunt for furniture in the ruined houses. We found half a dozen chairs and a table with a leg blown off, a stove punctured by shrapnel, and some crockery, which we picked up in a cellar of a building that must have been a happy home when it still had all of its three stories and the winding stairway, of which only parts were in place.

I climbed to the top of the structure, and looked into the rooms, from which the roof and ceiling had been blown off by shells. The furniture was still in the rooms and clothing was strewn all over the floor. Everything had been spoiled by rain and the shells and was on the verge of falling apart, but for all that it was still evident that it had been occupied by people of wealth.

One of the rooms must have been that of a young lady. In a dresser I found a pink

## WOUNDED AGAIN

evening gown and other articles of feminine apparel. I took it for granted that the owner of the dress was some beautiful girl, and I was still wondering what she might look like when Montgomery sneaked up the stairs and shouted to me to come down. I took the gown along and it was one of the treasures of the mess until I gave it to a peasant girl.

On the next floor must have been the room of the old man. We found several pipes and a pair of slippers, and a torn night robe. Back of this room was a sort of conservatory; it had been a pretty place once, but was that no longer. All the glass was broken and the flower pots and boxes lay pell-mell on the floor, with every plant in them dead. We examined the rooms on the ground floor and found that Tommie had been there before us. In the kitchen we made a haul, however. We found there a lot of dishes, three cut glass fruit platters, two soup tureens, some silver knives and forks, and two kitchen chairs. Then we went to the wine cellar but not a drop did we find. A lot of empties gave evidence that somebody had had a good time in that cellar. On leaving the house I spied a book. It turned out to be the Old and New Testament in Dutch, and in it was a card which I took to be that of the young lady. The Bible I sent to an old church-going friend and the card I kept myself.

We were about to drive off when we heard a dull boom in the distance, and a few seconds later a big shell screeched over us and exploded a block away. There was no time to lose, but as we made off Montgomery and the boys sang a little song from the West:

"He's a bold bad man and a desperado,
  Blows into town like a big tornado;
Steals all the money from the people in the
      land,
  He's a curly wolf at shooting with a gun in
      either hand."

The ruins of Ypres were a striking sight. It rather broke us up to see that beautiful and thrifty little town being flattened to the ground. There was an oppressive silence in the streets during the few moments when the detonation of guns and shells was not heard.

I looked at what had once been the famous

## WOUNDED AGAIN

Cloth Hall. I had been told by some French people that it was one of the finest buildings in France and Belgium, but now all its walls were hopelessly wrecked. The parts of the building that had not been blown up were so shaky that the concussion of nearby exploding shells would topple them over. There was no life in Ypres—nothing but rats, rats, and millions of them. I went into several houses which had been inhabited by people of wealth and everywhere met traces of the things which make for refinement—paintings, good furniture, and beautiful candelabras. Everything had been wrecked by the Hun. Before long the big guns of the German batteries started and their shells again began to level Ypres, for which they seemed to hold a hatred.

Shortly after that I had some trouble with the commanding officer, with the result that I was transferred to headquarters as a motor cycle dispatch bearer. Motor cycling on a good road is a pleasure, but on wet cobblestones and in the mud it is anything but that. It is impossible to go fast because that shakes the wheel all to pieces and is likely to break your neck, and when you go slow everybody grumbles. In a country such as Flanders, especially when the rainy spell is on, motor cycling keeps you covered with mud from head to foot, and dispatch riding is the very thing to keep you going day and night. Occasionally you run into a shell-hole in the dark and that means that your shins are always minus much of their bark. Another feature of dispatch riding is that you move constantly in zones where a shell may call you in at any moment.

But you aren't supposed to think in the Army, as I discovered again, when I had used my own judgment on one little trip I made. I delivered my message, but on my way back I had gone out of my way to see a pal who was at a wireless station further up the line.

I was having a chat with my friend when the signal officer came up in his car and saw me. That was enough. On my return to the base I was placed under arrest. In the morning a sergeant escorted me to the commanding officer.

That personage wanted to know what I had been doing ten miles out of my route. I

## WOUNDED AGAIN

told him that I had seen no harm in going to see my friend. The commanding officer could not see it that way. He led me to understand that he was the brains of the company and that I had no right to think at all—that I was there to ride. But I got even with him after I was made a commissioned officer.

A severe reprimand was all the punishment meted out to me. That same night I made a trip up to the lines and was going along at a fairly good speed when a scream and a crash about twenty-five yards ahead of me suddenly halted my progress. The next thing I knew was that I was lying against the bank on the side of the road some fifteen feet away from the motor cycle. A pain in my left shoulder told me what part of my body had struck the earth first, and when I tried to move my neck that pain grew more intense. I began to spit blood. My head started to buzz.

I noticed that my goggles were missing and since I had to send to England for them, I was not anxious to lose them. I saw them about twenty feet ahead of me and, finding my legs unsteady, I rolled towards them.

## THE FLYING FIGHTER

Before I reached them I fell flat twice. Shortly afterwards I was picked up and sent to the base hospital and from there to England.

Two months later I was back in France and attached to my old transport section. I found that there was considerable unrest among the boys for the reason that all of them were trying to get commissions. By this time also I had made up my mind to get into the Flying Corps. Scott and Beatty, friends of mine, had the same ambition, while others of the section were trying for other branches of the service—Jimmie Brown and Bud Shore for the artillery, Alexander McCollough for the machine gun section, and Dyas and Copman for the infantry.

We secured the necessary transfer forms, filled them up and sent them in. Meanwhile we were trying to get information on the nature of an officer's work in the different units. We had made up our minds to take a more serious view of army life, but before I heard anything from my application I was back on the job hauling coal and ammunition. The chances of getting into the Flying Corps

## WOUNDED AGAIN

seemed very remote. They seemed even remoter when on the first morning at the dumps behind the line a shell carried off poor old McConnell. A steel fragment went through his head. Poor Montgomery was severely wounded in the side and though he recovered he was never fit for service after that.

Three days later a Hun plane bombed the railhead. It dropped six bombs, but only two of them exploded. But the two did their work, killing five women and two children and a police sergeant and his horse. I looked up at the plane and wished that I could get at it for a few minutes. The anti-aircraft guns were working hard to down the machine, but did not touch it at all.

While in this sector, I saw lots of atrocities committed by the Germans. Although I could hardly believe all the stories I heard about them, there was no vestige of doubt left in my mind after seeing with my own eyes what the Huns were capable of doing.

I was driving up the road one afternoon about four o'clock. The sky was clouded and made the devastated country look all the more lonesome. Though ten miles behind the lines, the guns could be heard plainly and I felt lonely and homesick.

Beyond the little hill I spied a low red building with a cross in front of it, which I took to be a convent. Not being in a hurry, I thought that I would call on the French Fathers. They are always very interesting and knowing their language and customs I felt quite at ease with them.

In response to my knock at the door, a sister appeared. She asked me to come in and sent for one of the fathers. He was a white-haired old man and dressed in a long black robe with a heavy leather belt around his waist. A large crucifix was suspended from his neck.

We began to talk of the war and he told me of a lot of horrors he had seen—of children murdered by the Germans when they came to Belgium, of women outraged, and priests tortured for helping the Belgian soldiers. Then he took me to see the little convent and there I saw sights which still haunt me.

We came to a little chapel where nine little boys were kneeling. Looking at them I found that not one of them had his right hand. All

## WOUNDED AGAIN

were under twelve years old and the youngest was four. The little chap kept his right arm behind his back. It made the blood run cold in my veins and I thought of the children at home. I wanted some sort of revenge on the Huns.

One of the women in the chapel, the father told me, spent most of her time praying. Her little son had been killed and her daughter, a girl of seventeen years of age, had been taken away by the Huns.

Later I met many mothers to whom the same thing had happened. I also saw some women whose breasts and ears had been cut off. They had been tortured in the most cruel ways imaginable. When taking leave of the old father, I gave him all the money I had on me, forty francs, for which he thanked me. He also presented me with a little medal of the Virgin Mary and blessed me.

I went away with a heavy heart. The medal I added to my collection. My mother had given me a similar medal as had also my sister. An old priest who used to labor in the little Indian village on the Sarcee Reservation, back home in Canada, had also

## THE FLYING FIGHTER

given me one. I had four of them now, and carried them strung together with a safety pin, safely stowed away in my pocket.

On arriving in camp I was greeted by the sergeant-major with a torrent of bad language, and the order that I proceed immediately with my convoy to S., with the seven loads of ammunition that I was to unload and then return to the railhead. S. was a little place about a mile behind our first line, and known for the big shells the Huns used to put into it in their effort to blow up the ammunition dump.

I had been shelled there on a previous occasion and had just turned into the dump, where the mud was hub deep, when the shells started to fall. On one side of the road was a shed where the working parties detailed to help unload ammunition were sheltered from the weather. The first shell to-day fell into this shed, killing fourteen of the men. I blew my whistle as a signal for my men to take to cover. This they did by leaving their seats and getting under the lorries. We stayed there for two hours, with a shell coming every five minutes, which gave us ample time to work our way into the ditch along the main road. While the body of the lorries gave some protection, there is no telling what would have happened had one of the German shells hit a lorry loaded with ammunition or the depôt itself. As luck would have it, however, the shells fell everywhere but in the dump; so we thanked our stars, and when the bombardment was over unloaded the vehicles in record time. We had lost some time and went to the railhead at a good speed, where I was informed that the commanding officer wanted to see me.

# CHAPTER VII

### JOINING THE FLYING CORPS

I HAD visions of more trouble on reporting, but I was told by the officer that I was to fill out my papers for the Flying Corps, and that he would recommend my transfer to that branch of service. I could have kissed him right then and there so glad was I to have his consent and recommendation. I walked and rode eight miles up the lines to find a doctor I knew. He was at a field dressing station, but I was determined to reach him. One of the road sentries challenged me and I was told that he could not allow me to pass because a raid was on. I walked back and when out of sight of the picket cut across the fields on my hands and knees and in that manner got beyond him. I was taking a chance of being shot for disobeying the picket's orders, but I had to see the doctor that night.

## JOINING THE FLYING CORPS

I had not gone fifty yards when I heard "Halt! Who goes there?"

Since I had not seen anybody, the order was a shock to me. I nearly dropped from fright and answered in a weak little voice: "Friend."

The picket made me advance and now I could see his bayonet glisten in the moonlight. He wanted to know what I was doing there. But instead of taking a sympathetic view of it he began to curse me in the roundest of terms. He was a reasonable person, however, for after a little while he permitted me to go on. It so happened that I knew several men in his battalion and that seemed to remove all doubt from his mind that I was everything that I claimed to be.

After much hunting I found the field dressing-station, but the doctor was busy at the time dressing wounds.

One of the wounded men was a "Jock," or a Scotchman, who had been hit in the leg. The sergeant put a cigarette in his mouth and lit it; then he opened the man's coat and shirt and with a syringe as big as they use on horses he inoculated the "Jock" against tetanus poisoning, saying:

"Jock, I'll give you a hundred francs for that blighty." But the Scotchman replied:

"Ah, mon! it's worth that much for the thought of Scotland, and the blighty is worth it ten times. Why, I laid me doon in a shell hole in No Man's Land and put that foot up in the air and I waited for a hoor and a half before the bullet hit me. No, not for a thousand francs this blighty."

Another poor chap had a leg shattered, which had to be amputated, and no one offered him anything for that. But the doctor was very tender with him and soon he was on his way to the base whence he would be sent to England.

At about one o'clock in the morning the doctor was through and then I went to his dugout.

He seemed glad to see me. As he grabbed me he shouted:

"Why, you flea-bitten, horse-riding, buck-jumping old son-of-a-gun, how in the —— are you?"

The doctor had a little cache in his dugout

## JOINING THE FLYING CORPS

and out of that he took a bottle that contained something stronger than water. Then I told him what I had come for. I had known the doctor in the United States and he had not forgotten old times despite the fact that he was a Major. He looked at me quizzically after I had stated the nature of my errand, and said:

"I ought to examine your head. I am sure that you are plumb locoed. I won't sign your papers for the Flying Corps, for I think that you are close enough to death here."

We argued the point for a few minutes and then he signed them, nevertheless. I left the doctor with a promise that I would write to him and let him know how I got along.

That was not all the signing that had to be done. Somebody had to attest my character; another my mechanical knowledge and education. I thought that a friend of mine of the name of Starrett could attest to the latter, but he did not seem inclined to sign the paper. But after talking to him until I was blue in the face, he did as requested, and then I started back for my unit with his good luck wishes.

## THE FLYING FIGHTER

I arrived in camp at seven o'clock in the morning.

The day for which I had been hoping so long had finally come, so that, despite the exertions of the night, I felt in fine fettle. After cleaning up I went to the commanding officer and handed him the papers, now provided with the necessary signatures. A little later I had the consent of the Division General, and on the afternoon of the following day I reported to an air squadron for my mechanical examination.

A week later I was attached to a squadron as gunner on probation, and there the game began.

I was not yet an aviator. The commanding officer of the squadron told me that I would have to take a turn in the trenches for a week or so to learn what infantrymen had to go through. After that I was to do a week in the artillery, and still later I would have a week in the squadron school. After that he sent me to a battery then in the first line. There I was turned over to the Quartermaster to be fitted out with the necessaries for trench warfare, which consisted principally of a web

## JOINING THE FLYING CORPS

equipment for carrying everything one needs in a trench, pockets for ammunition, trenching tool, tin hat, mess kit, and gas helmet. The load was heavy enough for any pack mule. I had not joined the army to take the rôle of that animal, but it was my first step to escaping into the Flying Corps, and I would have gone through an ordeal ten times as bad to attain that end.

I reported at Headquarters at W. P., and from there I was taken into the front lines, and within a week I saw more soldiering than had been my lot since coming to France. I was given into the charge of the company commander, whose unit was just then on duty in the first-line trenches. The same night part of that company went out on a raid and I was one of them. We sneaked into No Man's Land and over to the Hun wire.

I had never received special training in that line of work, but I watched the others and did likewise. I had been equipped with a gun bayonet and knew how to throw a bomb.

The covering party was ahead of us, but before long we also were near the Hun wire. Just then a star shell went up and we all dropped on our stomachs. I was frightened to death as the machine guns started to work and mud and small stones began to fly all around us. And it seemed that all the machine guns in the Hun army were turned on me. The steel helmet began to hurt my head, for I was not used to it. The wet ground added to my discomfort, and I wished myself back in the old transport section. The wait on the wet grounds seemed interminable, but suddenly a number of explosions near by made me stop thinking entirely and the chap next to me whispered into my ears:

"Come on, boy! the covering party is bombing them."

We rushed over to the wire and I tore myself considerably getting through the entanglement. It was the first time that I had attempted so risky a business. But I seemed to have managed it well enough, for presently I stood on a German parapet.

I halted there for a moment and then seeing the other men inside the trenches I jumped in, landing in the bay back of a traverse all alone.

## JOINING THE FLYING CORPS

From near by came voices speaking German. I stood stock still for a minute. Shouts came and I knew that some of our fellows were mixing it with the enemy. The noise came from the left and seemed to be coming nearer.

The only thing that occurred to me then was to move towards the scene of the action. Just as I was rounding the corner of the traverse I came face to face with a Hun who was coming out of a dugout. For a moment the man stopped and then, muttering something about British swine, he started for me. I lunged with rifle and bayonet as hard as I could right for his stomach. The man fell back with a yell and would have pulled me into the dugout with him if I had not let go of the rifle. From behind I heard steps approaching. I took one of my hand grenades, pulled the pin, and was about to throw it at the forms which loomed in the dark, when I recognized the first one of them as the company commander. He said, "Come on, we've been here too long," and I thought of how much longer he would have stayed, if I had thrown the bomb. He was just coming around the corner of a bay in the trench, and behind him was a gang of Huns.

So far as we knew there were only two of us, and to judge by the noise they were making the Germans were coming in force. There was nothing to do but retreat, and with that in view we got over the top as quickly as possible, and started for our own trenches.

The whole action had taken place within about thirty minutes, but I was so excited over sticking the Hun that it seemed much longer. However, the exhilaration of my exploit soon left me when the boys told me that one of them, during a previous raid, had stuck thirty Germans. After that I felt that my one was not much. But I have seen that Hun fall back into his dugout a thousand times since then.

I learned that we had captured fifteen prisoners who were of the 227th Bavarians. They were sent back to headquarters to be examined, and were later taken to a prison camp in France or England.

One of the Germans spoke good English and I talked with him. He had lived in America until six months before the war, and

## JOINING THE FLYING CORPS

had worked in a butcher shop in Chicago. He wished that he was back there now.

I spent a part of that night toasting my shins in a dugout, drinking tea and eating bread with tinned Nova Scotian butter on it. After that I had a sound sleep, which was all too short, for early in the morning I had to join a party that was to bring out rations.

I was doing real soldiering now and had many a thrill. In the same afternoon I was going through a section of the trench when a shell from a German trench mortar landed in it and knocked in its wall. At the same spot our company commander, Captain Renville, was killed by a sniper shortly afterward. The company Sergeant-Major was the first to see him. The officer was still breathing but unconscious, and the Sergeant-Major yelled for stretcher-bearers on the double quick. The bearers ran up and we placed Captain Renville on the stretcher as carefully as we could. He was then taken to a dressing or first-aid station.

The occurrence made a deep impression upon us. The captain was a very fine man, and we regretted his misfortune. I was turn-

## THE FLYING FIGHTER

ing things over in my mind when I heard somebody behind me sob. Turning around I saw the Sergeant-Major in tears, and that caused me to cry myself. I had only known the captain for three days, but I had learned to like him very much. To the rest of the company the officer had been a brother and a leader.

We learned that night that Captain Renville had died, and this increased our sorrow. The men sat around gloomily, and the silence was only broken by solemn vows of future revenge. The resolutions that were heard would have put the fear of God into the Hun who fired the shot had he heard them. I guess that a lot of these vows were carried out. I wished to comfort the boys, but, you see, they wanted to be left alone to mourn their loss. It was not until the day before I left that any of them spoke much, outside of taking and giving orders. Some of us went to the funeral of Captain Renville, and there I felt as bad as if I had lost my own brother.

The scenes of the death and burial of Captain Renville were before my eyes most vividly all that day. I could still hear the bugle

## JOINING THE FLYING CORPS

sound the last post, and though I had heard it on several occasions before, and had listened to the last salute of the firing party, it seemed to make my blood run colder to-day than ever before. These honors meant recognition of the fact that a man had sacrificed all for King and Country. It was not my King nor was it my country, so I wanted my country's emblem with me when I died; for I never expected to get out of this mess alive. I always carried a large American flag with me for that purpose. Later, when I had become an officer, I hung it up in my hut. An Englishman came in one night and made rather caustic remarks about the U. S. A. Well, so far as that went, American men could take care of themselves, and when I told him we had once whipped England he grew angry and we mixed it. I gave him a black eye, and he came back and apologized to me in the morning.

I stayed the rest of the week in the trenches and had a number of unusual experiences. One day a Tommie with whom I had grown chummy, and who was trying to get into the Flying Corps, took me to an old trench from

## THE FLYING FIGHTER

which the retaining boards had been removed. He wanted to show me some German dead who had been buried in the bottom of the trench. There was hardly anything left except grinning skulls, but what impressed me most was the fact that their boots were still on their feet; I thought of the old saying: "He died with his boots on."

Then the man told me a story of two Irishmen to whom had been issued some of the bad boots that were sold to the British Government in the early days of the war. Some of these boots lasted three hours. As soon as they got wet, the soles, which were made of ground cork and glue pressed together, fell away and after that the man was barefooted.

The Irishmen, having no soles on their boots, decided to get a pair of the kind issued to the Hun soldiers. They asked the company commander if they could go out on patrol that night. The officer looked at them somewhat puzzled, and asked why they wanted to take such long chances on their necks.

Patrick answered that he wanted a pair of

## JOINING THE FLYING CORPS

Hun boots. The company commander laughed, and finally gave his consent.

That night the two went out separately, and when they got back into their own trench Pat said to Mike:

"Well, Mike, how did you make out?"

"Fine," said Mike; "the first one I killed had boots of my size."

With that he showed Pat the boots, asking at the same time: "And how did you make out?"

"Very badly," replied Pat; "I killed twelve of them, and not one of them had boots that would fit me."

"What size do you wear?" asked Mike.

"Eleven," said Pat.

"Well, begorra! It's not boots you want; it's the box they come in."

An Irish argument ensued and Pat was sent to the Quartermaster for a new pair of boots.

A few nights before I returned to Squadron Headquarters, I was sent into No Man's Land as a member of a working party that was to put in some new barbed wire and pickets. We carried the material through a sap which ran underneath our own wires, and when we got out of the sap we all felt as big as a house, and we were sure that the Huns would see us.

I could not imagine how they could miss me. Our conversation was in whispers, and that added considerably to that tired feeling. I suffered from nervous shock every time the mauls descended upon a picket. We worked fast and furiously, and I had lost much of my nervousness when somebody near me whispered:

"Get down! Get down!"

We all laid down right where we were and waited. The working party is protected by the patrol, and that patrol had warned us. We waited until we got another call that everything was clear and went to work again. After that every time a maul hit a post it sounded to me like a 12-inch gun. Presently the Huns started to send up star shells for the purpose of finding where the noise came from. By that time we were down again, of course. But the enemy took a chance with their machine guns in the direction from which the noise had come. The bullets went to one side of us, however. The firing did not

## JOINING THE FLYING CORPS

last long, and then we resumed our labor; but I heaved a sigh of relief when we were through with the job, and we were back in the second-line dugout with a kettle full of tea and some chuck.

Two days later I was called in by the commanding officer and ordered to return to my unit. His report of me, he said, he would send in by telephone. I surrendered my equipment, said good-bye to the boys I had met, and started for Squadron Headquarters. I had gone about two miles on my way back when I passed something that resembled a house. Part of the chimney was shot off, and the windows were all broken. The ruin was similar to many others one could find around that part of the country.

Of a sudden the front of the structure slid to one side and a roar like a clap of thunder came out of it. Then followed a burst of smoke and a glimpse of the long, great barrel of a heavy gun settling on the recoil, and then the front of the house slid back—camouflage. For some minutes there was an awful ringing in my ears, and I had to hunt for my cap, which had been blown off my head. I found

## THE FLYING FIGHTER

it under the leafless branches of a tree across the road, and near it were the bodies of four small birds which had been killed by the concussion.

## CHAPTER VIII

### MY FIRST FLIGHT

Upon my arrival at squadron headquarters I reported to the commanding officer, who called in one of the flight commanders. The two of them discussed for a while as to what pilot was to take me up on a trial trip, and when this serious business had been disposed of, I was sent to the quartermaster of the aerodrome to be fitted out with the requisites of the flyer. These consist of a helmet, leather coat, fur gloves, and goggles.

The pilot with whom I was to fly told me to take the front seat of the machine and strap myself in. While I was attending to that my nerves seemed a little bit unruly. The moment for which I had hoped so much was come at last, but my sensations were not exactly what I had imagined they would be.

As I fastened each strap around me the risks of aviation became more real. Though

## THE FLYING FIGHTER

I had often dwelt on the fact that there are no landing places in the air, the straps brought to me full realization that whatever happened to the airplane would happen to me. There was no getting away from the machine in case something went wrong.

But there was no time for philosophizing. The pilot took his seat behind me, strapped himself in, tested various levers and contrivances; in the meantime somebody started the motor of the plane running.

I noticed that several men were holding the machine back until the propeller should have gained the speed necessary to give us a good start across the field.

I do not remember whether the pilot gave the signal that he was ready by word or by a gesture. Anyway, of a sudden the machine started to move, began to "taxi" across the field, and gained momentum with each instant.

It is hard to describe the sensation I had when the kite was finally in motion. I remember that the pilot opened the engine out and that the earth seemed to roll from under us, though the bumping of the wheels on the

## MY FIRST FLIGHT

ground reminded me that we were still "taxiing."

Of a sudden the bumping ceased and we seemed suspended in mid-air. But the wheels hit some other high places, showing that as yet we were not off the ground. Once more the machine was being supported on its wings. I hoped that the wheels would touch ground again, but hoped in vain.

The motor was speeding up now and the peculiar swaying motion of the machine left no doubt in my mind that we had left the ground for good.

I noticed that the airplane was flying steadily enough, but for all that I felt the uneasiness which is experienced by the person who is at sea for the first time. The slightest departure of the machine from its horizontal course threatened to upset my stomach.

But before long interest in the things underneath me overcame that sensation. The earth was receding in the most peculiar manner. I told myself that we were going up, but still the idea that remained uppermost in my mind was that the earth was dropping away from us.

## THE FLYING FIGHTER

We began to climb up and up. I was beginning to enjoy this when of a sudden the engine stopped. My heart went into my mouth. And I said to myself, 'Willie, you're a dead one.' I expected to fall. But the machine continued on an evel keel, and from back of me came two sharp raps. Then I was sure I was gone.

I looked around and saw the pilot smiling. He was saying something which I had great difficulty in understanding. But from his lips I read the question:

"How do you like it?"

I replied that I liked it well enough, and judged from the searching look in the eyes behind the goggles that the pilot was very much interested in ascertaining the state of my nerves. The result of his scrutiny must have been satisfactory to him, for presently he began to point out the objects on the ground, which was now far below us. We were then some eight thousand feet above the ground.

The pilot drew my attention to lines on the ground—mere pencil marks—and he told me that these were the trenches and communica-

## MY FIRST FLIGHT

tion ditches, and I thought how much safer the boys in the trenches were, even with the mud and rats. The lines stretched out as far as the eye could reach, and were parallel in the main, though here and there they diverged a little to come closer to one another at some other place. Over and near the lines wide puffs of smoke appeared. They were caused by exploding shells. I began to listen for the detonations, but the noise of the motor made it impossible for me to hear anything else.

So long as the puffs of smoke stayed near the ground and the trenches, all was well, I concluded. But I remembered the Hun aviator's fate at Ypres, and wondered how long it would be before those beautiful little smoke puffs would come nearer to us.

While I was still wondering a flash ahead of us rent the air. It was yellow and intense. The next moment a round powder puff took its place, and from this began to curl in all directions smoke ribbons which the fragments of the exploding shell were drawing after them.

I looked around at the pilot. He said nothing, but held up two warning fingers, while

## THE FLYING FIGHTER

over his face went an expression of disdain.

Four other shrapnel shells exploded near us, and there was now no doubt in my mind that "Archie" was very busy with his anti-aircraft battery.

The Hun aircraft batteries, however, did not seem to be as greatly interested in us as they might have been, and after a while their efforts to bring us down ceased.

I was once more able to watch things beneath us. The earth looked flat now. Hill and dale had disappeared. We sailed over a forest and I found that it looked like a lawn. Only its darker green separated it from the remainder of the landscape. The farmhouses were the size of a match box and the fields around them seemed parts of a checkerboard. Men could not be seen at all. Two little towns over which we flew looked about a foot square.

I was enjoying this very much when of a sudden the engine stopped once more. Somehow I had learned to look upon that motor as something human, and I found myself unconsciously appealing to it to start again. I knew, of course, that the machine could volplane—glide—to earth, but I was not so sure

## MY FIRST FLIGHT

that this particular pilot, despite his great reputation, was really the man to bring me safely back to earth.

The list of the machine forward made another severe attack upon my nerves. I surmised that the pilot intended to glide. What I feared most, however, was that he might attempt to do some of the fancy tricks aviators are fond of, especially when they have novices aboard. There might be somersaults, just plain or corkscrew fashion, and I was quite sure that anything of the sort would be too much for me.

But this did not seem to be the intention of the pilot. I had hardly found comfort in that thought when I noticed that the speed of the machine was now so terrific that the wire stays began to scream and whistle. The sensation of great speed overwhelmed me. Everything began to revolve about me, and I had to keep my eyes off the earth in order not to grow sick. It was not the motion of the machine alone that caused this sensation, but the great speed at which the earth seemed to be coming up to meet us.

Minutes seemed hours long, and with each

second my prayers that this would soon be over grew more fervent. I was suffering all the tortures man ever imagined.

Of a sudden the machine lurched. The increased pressure against the plane could be felt by a tautness that went over every part of it, my own body and mind included. The next moment I noticed that the wire stays were no longer singing, and then, to my great surprise, I noticed that we were directly above the aerodrome.

The realization that this trip would soon be over was a great relief. But another fear seized me. We were not far from the ground now, but were still going at such a speed that the machine coming in contact with the ground would certainly be smashed; so, at least, I thought.

That was not the case, however, though the bounce we got when the wheels first touched showed me that it was indeed well to be strapped into the seat. The strain of my body against the leather was such that the straps creaked, and I would have been catapulted out of the machine had it not been for the safeguarding strap.

## MY FIRST FLIGHT

After the first bounce the machine traveled another short distance on its planes, hit the ground once more, rose again, and then taxied up to the shed.

I unstrapped myself and then climbed out of the machine. I was glad to be once more on solid ground even though it did heave a bit.

The impression that my first flight made upon me was shown by a dream I had that night. I dreamed that I was up in the air higher than anybody had ever been before, and that the machine suddenly broke up into small parts. I was plunging down trying to catch these parts and was just about to hit the ground when I discovered that I was on the floor near my bunk.

Next morning I learned that the Hun shrapnel had not been as innocuous as I had imagined. There were several holes in the planes of the machine which must have been made by the contents of the shell which exploded behind us, and which I could not see from my seat in front. But old "Archie" had been a little off-color in his shooting, as he generally is.

I was discussing our trip with the pilot who

had taken me up, Lieut. R——, when an orderly came out and told me that I was to report at headquarters. There I was told that I was to be sent to a battery of sixty-pounders to learn what I could about artillery.

The next stage in my training as aviator was accomplished in that battery.

Much of my life, while attached to the battery, I spent in a dugout, which was comfortable enough; besides, the bugs had been trained to leave strangers alone—so, at least, the Sergeant-Major said. But in that, as in other things, he was mistaken. The insects took a violent liking to me and inside of three days I had the finest collection of them the battery could boast of.

I made the acquaintance of a new sport while with the battery. A saucer serves for an arena. Into this one puts a kootie and a flea. A vicious fight results and on the outcome of that the boys bet. The combat generally ends in favor of the flea.

During the third night of my stay with the battery, about eleven o'clock, I was awakened by a heavy explosion. I started to my feet, but before I could find myself another

## MY FIRST FLIGHT

explosion came. I made for the surface and just as I reached there another bang close by shook me off my feet. In my hurry to get back into the dugout I missed the first step and landed unceremoniously at the bottom. I flew through the sacking which serves as a door and lit on one of the gunners who slept in the corner of the dugout.

The man was so used to night bombardments that he did not mind the noise of the shells. But he thought differently of the disturbance I was causing. His flow of language was very sulphurous and included a peremptory command that I shut the door. He opined that it was a shame to send a "mutt" like me down to a battery to create trouble and attract gun fire to a gang of peaceful gunners.

The battery was shelled for three nights running and I was blamed for it. Before my arrival the battery had been living peacefully enough, they said, and while they granted that I had made no deal with the Germans, they still insisted that I was a Jonah. Whereupon I returned to my little two by twice corner and went to sleep.

## THE FLYING FIGHTER

I was put to work, however. I assisted in loading one of the big guns and as a special favor I was permitted to yank the lanyard a couple of times. Then they tried to explain sighting to me. I heard lengthy expositions of errors in elevation and the like, and somebody said a great deal in explanation of loading, relaying, fire and what not before I left.

I also learned that the fire was being directed from the ground from what the battery commander called the O. P., or observation post. He sent me up to that post with one of the spotters. We reached it on our hands and knees and found that its site was an old tree stump to which a telephone line had been laid. From that spot the observation man directed the fire by means of a telephone. His work consisted of telephoning to the battery commander whether the fire was short or high, or fell to the side of the object aimed at.

The language of the observation post was Chinese to me at first. I could not make out what they meant by "No. 1 gun, two minutes, five degrees right."

After that No. 2 gun would take a whirl at it as the next correction indicated. That cor-

## MY FIRST FLIGHT

rection might be: "No. 2 gun, one minute, eight degrees far."

It was all Dutch to me, but it was interesting to watch it. I afterwards found out that the fire spotter sometimes worked in connection with airplanes when shrapnel was being used, the duties of the ground observer in that case being to determine the height at which the shrapnel was exploding. The aerial observer also had to report on the effect of the fire. Nobody had explained to me so far why I had been attached to the battery and nobody ever did, but I surmised they wanted me to get up some acquaintance with artillery practice. Some day no doubt, if I live long enough, I would have to spot shrapnel while on the wing, and my apprenticeship with artillery would then have some value.

To observe artillery fire from above was the very thing I wanted to do, and I made up my mind that the corrections I sent down should be as accurate as possible. With that in mind I absorbed as much of artillery technique as I could. I was anxious to get back to the Flying Squadron in the hope that I would get another flight right away. On arriving at headquarters I had the satisfaction of being told by the commanding officer of the squadron that I was doing fine; but to this remark he added that I was to keep it up and then sometime or other I might be a real birdman.

The next week I spent in learning a great deal about the Lewis gun. I was taken to a range and taught how to use it, how to remedy its jams, change broken cartridge guide springs, and apply the immediate action on an empty drum.

The gun I was handling had all the defects which I might have to overcome in the air, and I will say that my course on the range was very thorough. Later, I learned how to fix the "double feed jam," change extractors, regulate the action of the bolt and do the many other things one has to know in order to keep a machine gun running.

I put in a very busy week, especially since in addition to my study of the Lewis gun I had to continue artillery observation practice. I discovered that spotting artillery fire while moving about on an airplane was not so simple as I had imagined. The things I

## MY FIRST FLIGHT

was supposed to learn were piling up rapidly, moreover. By the end of the week I had also been introduced to wireless telegraphy. I worked fourteen hours each day.

## CHAPTER IX

#### MY FIRST HUN

The next trip I made aloft was made as gunner in a fighting airplane. We were on patrol for three hours, and I had a busy time of it trying to keep my mind on the gun and flying at the same time. On my next trip I spent a hundred rounds from a Lewis gun at a target and the same day I was sent as gunner* on another patrol.

We had been up for an hour, when the pilot spotted a Hun battery and gave its direction to some of our guns. We were then about six miles behind the German line. All went well for a time until I saw another machine at about our own level, to which I called my pilot's attention. Though the other craft was at least a mile away the pilot recognized it immediately as a Hun. He began to tap out something on the wireless key which, as I afterwards learned, was a message to the

## MY FIRST HUN

battery with which we were working to cease firing. The hostile machine was also an observer and the flash from our guns would have shown its pilot where our battery was located.

The thought that there was a Hun in the air and that we might have to meet him gave me a nervous thrill since I somewhat doubted my ability to handle a machine gun. The man in the other machine might be much more proficient than I; and, while I had broken bottles on the range, fired on the outline of a Hun plane on the ground for practice, and done other trial stunts, I had never before tried issues with a real live Hun.

But I found a great deal of comfort in the fact that my pilot was a good man (he had been decorated for bravery) and I made up my mind that I was not going to disappoint him. He had shown that he had faith in me, and for that reason I had myself well in hand when the German machine came nearer to us.

But it was not our business to fight down the hostile machine. We were observers. It was rather risky, moreover, to take up a fight with a Hun above his own territory, where a forced landing would have resulted in our being made prisoners of war. Consequently we started for home, but Fritz saw fit to follow us.

We were over No Man's Land when finally we turned on him, and I got ready to work the machine gun. I knelt down in the seat and when we were close enough the pilot turned around and gave me the signal to fire. But the Hun was miles past, and I wondered if the pilot thought that I was the champion trap shot of the world. There were no synchronized machine guns in those days, and to shoot through the propeller meant of course that there would be a sudden landing since the bullets would splinter its blades to pieces. We came alongside of each other and I had put a drum of cartridges in the gun and was in the act of aiming at the Hun machine when something hit a strut alongside of my head. A glance in the direction of the strut showed me that a bullet had gone through. Quick as a wink I pulled the trigger and the little gun began to jump and bounce about on its mounting.

## MY FIRST HUN

What the effect of my fire would be I was anxious to know. The racket made by the machine gun was deafening, and since its muzzle was directly above my pilot the man had to crouch down into the cockpit. But he, too, was interested in seeing what I was doing and after a few moments he sat up again.

I was shaking with excitement by now. The machine gun was spitting bullets at a fast rate, but on the Hun plane everything remained in order. The two machines were keeping to a parallel course and I was beginning to fear that my aim was too poor to bring down our opponents, who were meanwhile keeping up their fire.

Of a sudden the enemy machine lurched forward. Then something detached itself from it. It was the form of a falling man.

My excitement reached its height. My aim had been good after all. As I saw the body speed towards the ground, turning over and over again, a sensation of sickness seized me. So intense was this that I hoped the next enemy would get me in order that I might not have to go through this agony again.

## THE FLYING FIGHTER

Meanwhile the pilot had seen the falling Hun. There was a smile on his face as he shouted:

"Damn good!"

The Hun machine had curved back to the rear of its own line and we also made a turn during which we ascertained that the man had fallen inside of his own lines, having hit the ground behind the reserve position.

Something had gone wrong with the Hun machine, however. After a while it began to volplane rapidly; finally, it hit the ground with such force that the wings left the body of the machine.

While I was taking the empty ammunition drum from the machine, the pilot sent something over the wireless and before long our battery was at work again.

When our period of patrol was over we went home and made a good landing. The other men crowded around us. They had seen the fight and were eager to shake hands with us. I pretended not to be excited, but I wanted to get up and shout to the world that I had brought down a Hun in the air, and

## MY FIRST HUN

assisted the pilot looking over the machine to find what damage the Hun machine gunner had done to it. We found that he had eight hits to his credit. A ninth bullet had gone through the pilot's leather coat at the shoulder.

The commanding officer of the squadron also congratulated both of us.

I confess that I was rather pleased with myself, and at the mess that night my brother sergeants contributed not a little to that feeling. One of them, however, a Cockney, proceeded promptly to take some of the conceit out of me.

"Ay, mytes, look at that bloke! 'e don't 'alf fauncy 'isself, cause 'e pitched down a bloomin' 'un," he remarked, laughingly.

Since he had not done even that much, I could not see why he should put in his jaw, and so I came back at him with, "Well, I don't see any medals on you for anything you ever did." He lost his temper, but the rest of the boys soon brought him to his senses.

It was not long before some of the other sergeants made me feel that they did not like me any too well. Several of them remarked

## THE FLYING FIGHTER

that I was a Yankee, and the way of saying it was uncomplimentary. Finally the Sergeant-Major put a stop to the argument, but before he did this I learned that it did not pay to argue with sergeant-majors when you are a junior.

The following week, while on reconnaissance about thirty miles behind the German lines, our machine and another were flying along merrily when we were tackled by six Germans. The odds were against us, so we headed for our own lines at an elevation of about six thousand feet.

The Huns, however, had made up their minds that we should not get away if they could prevent it, and they attacked us. Some of them were trying to get ahead of us, while others sought to get directly underneath us, so that they could reach us the better with their machine guns. One of the machines got over us. In fact, they overlooked no point of vantage to put an end to our career. Finally, one of the Huns, who seemed more daring than the others, made straight for the other machine. I began to fire. After a while the tracers hit his engine and then he

## MY FIRST HUN

glided to earth. I cursed my luck for having only disabled him.

The other machines were still flying around us, though by this time in larger circles. Although we were now near our own lines, they kept pegging away at us and some of their bullets kept spinning past us dangerously close.

Just as we got over our lines, the Huns made another big try to get us. Our machines separated in order to not give the Germans a chance to attack us together. Two of them went for my machine while the other three attacked the other. I fought my opponents at long range, hoping to hold them off in that manner. But they were energetic and daring enough. They closed in on us and the rattle of their machine guns could be heard above the roar of my engine, so close were they.

The Huns decided to try other tactics. One of them started to climb while the other kept on a level with us. Not one of them remained in any position very long. Of a sudden the Hun machine which had managed to get well above us began to dive, and as he did so its

## THE FLYING FIGHTER

gunner landed a bullet in the shoulder of my pilot, Captain Robertson.

I feared that the Captain had been disabled, and was ready to jump into his place. If he lost consciousness the machine would be out of control, and in that case it would have been the last trip for both of us.

Captain Robertson remained conscious. He seemed unable, however, to keep control of the machine. We began to descend rapidly towards Hun land and I had visions already of being captured and made a prisoner of war.

To find out in what state the pilot was I shouted at him. Instead of saying a word, however, he pointed up at one of the Huns who had just passed us. That signal, as I presently came to understand, was intended to show me that we were to dive to the ground.

A grand nose dive came. It was made at so steep an angle that the oil rushed out of the breather pipes and covered my face. It also blinded my goggles so that I was obliged to waste time in wiping them off with my handkerchief.

But that was soon done. There was a whole

## MY FIRST HUN

drum of cartridges, on the machine, and as the Hun came to my level again I let fly at him. I saw him raise himself, then he dropped back in his seat—dead.

With that machine out of the way the pilot pulled ours up once more, and soon we were headed for home.

Captain Robertson was getting weaker all the time, however, and I began to doubt whether we would get over the line. In the course of our fight with the Hun machines, we had gone back over the German lines, as I now discovered, and our speed had fallen off alarmingly.

I am not much of a praying man, but right there I said the little prayer my old mother had taught me. Meanwhile, I kept my eyes open for the remaining Hun, who was still near us. I hoped that he would decide to stay away for I had only one drum of ammunition left—47 rounds. He was obliging enough to do this.

But now we were again within range of the German anti-aircraft batteries, which began to fire at us. They hammered away industriously, but luck was with us.

# THE FLYING FIGHTER

We crossed the lines without further injury and landed at a French aerodrome. Though disabled, my pilot made a very fine landing. He was bandaged up by the French and sent by motor car to the hospital. I telephoned to the commanding officer of the squadron to tell him what had happened and he sent another pilot down to get the machine. On our arrival at the Squadron aerodrome I was welcomed by the commanding officer and learned that the other machine which had accompanied us had been helped out of a tight fix by two French machines.

Between the three of them they had brought down two of the Huns, the third having made a rapid retreat as a captive balloon of ours had observed.

From the same captive balloon my fight had also been seen, and its observer reported that the machine whose pilot I had shot had come down with a crash behind the Hun lines.

My month of probation was not yet over and such time as I did not spend in the air had to be devoted to study. Finally I was sent to H. where at the headquarters of the Royal Flying Corps I was told that I was to

## MY FIRST HUN

proceed to England to get my officer's kit, this being the first intimation that I had been given a commission. Needless to say, I was as proud as a peacock, and the prospects of seeing England again increased my happiness. There was no holding me, and I blew myself to a wine dinner in a little French hotel. I was a stranger and for that reason had to celebrate all alone. The celebration ceased on the arrival of my train.

# CHAPTER X

### MY COMMISSION

I ARRIVED in London too late in the evening to report at headquarters, and decided to have a look at Piccadilly Circus, which I had no trouble in finding this time. I also met two boys from home, who were on leave, and the three of us went all over town, finishing up at Murray's Club, which was then open all night.

After a short period of enjoyment, I settled down to business, getting ready, among other things, my officer's equipment. The uniform I now put on impressed me very much more than did the one I had donned in Canada. It was a novelty to have the Tommies and non-commissioned officers salute me. But that sensation soon wore off; there were so many of them that my right arm was nearly paralyzed by night time.

There is nobody who can take the conceit

## MY COMMISSION

out of a man as well as one's friends. I had my picture taken in my uniform and sent photographs to friends at home who promptly discovered that the old uniform had fitted me much better. A week later I was back on my way to France, meeting at the port of embarkation a pal from my end of the world, James Newton. He was very much surprised to see that I was an officer now, but said that he would not salute me if I were a general.

I had orders to report to the embarkation officer in France, and he sent me to one of the aircraft parks further inland. The commanding officer of the squadron to which I had been detailed gave me what seemed to be a chilly reception.

"I don't know anything about you at all, old chap," he said, as he sized me up. I was dead tired and hungry and did not care whether he knew anything about me or not.

"Well, give me something to eat," I said, "and a bed for the night. To-morrow we can call up headquarters and find out where I am to go."

I managed to get some food all right, but no place to sleep. The commanding officer of the squadron spent a good part of that evening getting in touch with headquarters, and when at eleven o'clock he had finally managed to do that I was packed into a motor car and sent to the headquarters in question. It was a three hours' drive to get to my destination, and I was almost frozen when I got there.

At headquarters I met a good old staff colonel, who did his best to make me comfortable, so that soon I was sitting beside a fire and had a glass of Scotch beside me. A little later they had found a nice room for me and I was asleep in less time than it takes to tell it.

During the day I was called into the office of the Colonel and was then given my route orders and instructed to report to a squadron in the South. I had been attached to a squadron in the part of France to which I was going and I wondered whether my orders would send me there again.

I should have liked to get back to that squadron, but it was not to be.

The commanding officer of the squadron to which I was attached gave me to understand that his was the crack organization of the corps, but they all do that. After that he told me minutely what he expected me to do, and, believe me, it was a whole lot.

But he seemed quite nice about it, and so I made up my mind to do my best to satisfy him.

About a quarter of a mile away from the aerodrome was a little wood into which the Boches were in the habit of putting shells all through the day and night. In the woods was an Armstrong hut which was assigned to me as my quarters, and my real flying life had begun. Next morning I was given a set of maps of the country we had to work in and, from the number issued to me, I arrived at the conclusion that this squadron covered most of France. I was also assigned to a pilot by the name of Smith.

It was in this squadron that I received my first nickname; it happened in this manner. The squadron, being English, its men followed the English custom of having breakfast at seven in the morning, lunch at one in the afternoon, tea at four, and dinner at eight or nine in the evening. The breakfast was very good, but lunch was a cold meal with canned tongue or a cold ham and salad. In the parts of the world that I come from we have the habit of calling the midday meal dinner, and it was the big meal of the day. For that reason I found it hard to get used to this cold meal. I felt the need of something warm in the middle of the day, so I went to A. and there bought myself about fifteen cans of pork and beans. The cook used to warm these up for me for lunch, and it was not long before I had the squadron eating pork and beans. That led to my being known to the commanding officer as "Beanface." The name stuck.

Before long I had another nickname—Casey. That name came to me from a rag time record on our phonograph popularly known as "Casey Jones," the same Casey Jones who went down on the *Robert E. Lee*. I learned the thing by heart and used to sing it at the weekly concerts we gave our men. The concert always was a big affair and we used to get a battalion band to play for us. But my Casey Jones song continued to be a feature of the concerts, hence the nickname.

## MY COMMISSION

As I said, my pilot's name was Smith. I called him "Smithie." His other name I never learned.

Pilot Smithie was a good sort and aside from having a wholesome fear of the Hun "Archies," he was a brave boy, as I soon found out.

We were assigned to a patrol and for a week nothing of much importance happened. On a Sunday afternoon, while aloft, I noticed that the aircraft sign intended to warn us of danger had out the figure "8." Looking in the direction indicated by the arrow on the ground I saw eight German machines on reconnaissance behind our lines. Our "Archie" guns were hammering at them and before long one of the Hun machines detached itself from the flock and headed for home.

The machine I was in was about a thousand feet above him and as the Hun came towards us my pilot began to play for position so that I might get a good shot at him. He managed to get above the Hun machine, and as it came past us its gunner started to work his machine gun. I returned his fire, and for the first two drums of cartridges no result was obtained. But with the first half of the third drum I killed the gunner.

We then closed in on the man who was flying the machine. He looked at me as I took aim and I hated to shoot him. But as I thought of the chances I would have if I were in his boots I just naturally pulled the trigger and hit him with a string of about thirty cartridges.

His machine turned towards our lines of a sudden and then headed down to earth. Then it began to spin, there was a little puff of dust as he hit, and it was all over.

My pilot was overjoyed and I was quite proud myself, but I thought of what it meant to be shot at nine thousand feet above the ground and of the crash when the machine landed. What a finish!

When we were through with patrol work, we returned to headquarters, and that night the dead Hun looked at me as he had done in the afternoon; as a result I slept very little.

In the long run flying gets as monotonous as riding a motor car, and one soon gets to look upon it as hard work. It *is* hard work.

## MY COMMISSION

I have found my nerves strung to such a pitch that I could do nothing for a minute or so, and at such times I would chew my lead pencils.

My student period was not yet over. There was still much to learn. It was not alone the question of how to handle a machine gun or even the airplane itself; the service which the aviator is expected to render is complicated and intensive in its many details. For instance, so far I had learned little of what is known as Contact Control, the purpose of which is to keep in touch with advancing infantry, tabulate its progress, and then report to headquarters. Each battalion or other unit advancing has a call of its own when it wants to signal. This is transmitted to the observer aloft by means of a ground-sheet and shutter, the message being conveyed by means of dots and dashes. The airplane observer is expected to take this message and relay it by wireless to headquarters. When convenient he will fly over headquarters every fifteen minutes to either drop message bags or report in person.

To study that system I was sent with my

## THE FLYING FIGHTER

pilot to a French aerodrome. We began to map out the country behind it, and then practiced this system of signalling with troops detailed for the purpose.

I will explain here briefly what the organization of the average flying squadron is. It generally has from four to seven machines to a flight and from two to four flights, and each flight is commanded by a flight commander, who generally has the rank of captain. This officer is also charged with the duties of the commanding officer in an administrative sense. He is empowered to punish his rank and file. But he is responsible to the officer commanding the squadron for orders.

The commanding officer of my squadron was an Irish Catholic, and he was to us a sort of Father Confessor. He went to church every Sunday morning in a little village near our camp. Usually we who were Catholics went along. The commanding officer had a real prayer book, which to me was quite a novelty. I had not been to church for so long that I did not remember much about it. But it soon came back.

## MY COMMISSION

The old Father was an army chaplain and his little church was about five miles behind the lines. The people who attended were poor but proud, as most of the real French people seem to be. They felt the war quite badly, but despite that they had masses said for their dead sons, husbands, and brothers. They all showed a wonderful spirit, as was evidenced by the firm voices in which they said their prayers for those who were fighting.

We invited the Father to come over to the squadron and have dinner with us, and one night he came. Before leaving our camp he blessed our machines. After that we saw quite a lot of him, though he was very busy with the troops under his care, whom he called his flock, and with the peasants, who all went to him when they were in trouble.

There was a large Hun aerodrome at Cambrai, about fifty miles from our camp. It had been decided to bomb this. Three machines were to go. Of the three selected mine was one. It was a beautiful evening and the raid was supposed to be made that night.

We put on our duds and piled into the

machine and soon we were up in the air. Though it was dark, there was no danger of losing our way as the roads show plainly at night as well as lakes and rivers, which look like silver, and the lines were being lit up by star shells. From above, these lights could be seen from a long way off and when many of them were up it was a pretty sight indeed. The star shells burst very much as did a large shell, and when many of them go up at one time they furnish a splendid pyrotechnic display.

On this night the front was quite busy. The star shells lighted up great stretches, and the wonder of it was heightened by the flash of guns and exploding shells. We crossed the Hun lines at a good height and were soon behind them. As we went over their "Archies" we found that our coming was known. Shrapnel began to burst below us, but our machine went straight over and before long we were near our mark. The pilot shut off the power and glided down to within 500 feet of the Hun aerodrome; then he pulled the plugs that liberated the bombs.

As the bombs exploded everything below

## MY COMMISSION

us jumped into action. Searchlights began to flit about and tried to find us. More shrapnel reached up for us.

The other two machines after "laying their eggs" had started upward again, but my pilot seemed to have some trouble in starting his motor. We were still going down, as I could tell by the searchlights, and it seemed to me that we were dangerously near the ground when the engine suddenly began to work.

We flew very low over the ground for some distance before we had speed enough to "zoom." But after that we lost no time recrossing the Hun lines, which we did at an elevation of about 5,000 feet.

When we arrived at the aerodrome the pilot told me that we had had a narrow escape and that the engine had started again just in the very nick of time. Otherwise we would have been obliged to land in the terrain of the Huns at Cambrai.

I thanked my stars that I had not known it at the time, for I am sure I would have died then and there of heart failure.

About a week later I was flying behind the Hun lines with a pilot named Knight, when, on turning around to go back to our line, the engine slowed down.

Knight did not succeed in starting up again, though he tried hard. We were going down, down, down—towards the Hun lines. Soon the machine guns started to work on us from the ground. We were in a terrible situation. I had shouted several times at the pilot, but getting no answer from him finally looked around.

The pilot was gone!

But he had not fallen out as I feared. My frantic yells finally reached him, and then I discovered that he was at the bottom of the cockpit trying to fix the throttle of the engine, which had broken.

It was easier to reach the throttle from my position, and more than once I had thought out just that emergency. Now I was to put my theory into action. Taking off my heavy flying coat, and supporting myself on my head and shoulders on the floor of the machine, I reached around the foot-board and opened the throttle. That started the motor again and once more we avoided being made prisoner by the Huns.

## MY COMMISSION

So far so good, but in reaching down to get at the throttle I had wedged myself between some stays and trusses from which I found it impossible to extricate myself.

The remainder of the trip to our aerodrome I made upon my head.

By the time we reached camp the pains in my neck were almost unbearable and for the next week I walked around with a stiff neck.

The work we were doing was very interesting and I got my full share of it. There were also days on which we had little to do and then we would go to a little country house nearby to visit two of the nicest girls I've ever known. When there was little to do up in the air we would go to a nearby battery and help the crew a little and learn as much as we could.

# CHAPTER XI

### BATTERING THE HUN

I FOUND artillery work most attractive, both on the ground and when up in the air. I used to control fire by sending the necessary corrections to the batteries by wireless.

Aerial control of artillery fire works something like this: Let us say that I am up on patrol and see a Hun gun shooting. To stop him I call artillery headquarters by wireless and if the enemy gun happens to be a registered target, in other words a gun whose site is located, headquarters will telephone up to the battery which has the registration—meaning the necessary data on elevation and horizontals.

In a very short time after that Mr. Hun quits his funny work.

If it should happen that the Hun is making himself a general nuisance and the battery has not been located, I call up general headquarters and let them know that I want to "strafe" that Hun. Headquarters then lets me pick a battery of guns with which to work and I get in touch with that battery.

I can reach them with wireless but they cannot communicate with me in that manner, so that I depend upon their signals, which are strips of cloth on the ground, placed in certain formations. There would be no difficulty in receiving wireless on an aeroplane were it not for the noise of the motor and the vibrations of the machine, both of which make all known methods of receiving wireless messages absolutely impossible. But the signals on the ground answered the same purpose though they were not by any means so convenient.

I call the battery and let them know who I am, and ask them if they will "take on the shoot."

As soon as the battery has signalled to me that they will, I indicate by map co-ordinates, as far as is possible, the target's position. When the battery is ready to fire, another signal is put out, letting me know that they are ready to fire, so that I may be able

## THE FLYING FIGHTER

to watch the effect of the shot after it has left the gun.

The first shots as a rule fall wide of the mark, and I have only heard of one instance in which an aerial observer was able to plant a shell right in the middle of a Hun battery the first time. And I am inclined to believe that that was accident entirely.

But let us say that the first shot falls three hundred yards short of the target. In that case the battery is told by wireless that it must rectify its elevation accordingly. But it is not so simple while up in the air to determine just how far a shell has fallen wide of the mark. It is possible only by drawing imaginary circles around the Hun battery, each of these circles representing one hundred yards. If an error has been made in this calculation the next shot will show it.

When finally the shells fall within a hundred yards or so of the battery it becomes necessary to draw smaller circles, 50 yards, 25 yards and 10. These circles are named by letters of the alphabet. Let us say that the distances, 200, 100, 50, 25 and 10 yards are known to the gunners in the battery as

## BATTERING THE HUN

L, M, N, O, P. They are also bisected by figures from 1 to 12, 12 being due north and 6 due south, while 3 and 9 are respectively east and west.

If a shot falls in the 50-yard circle and northeast of the battery, I would in that case send down to the battery's fire control the message N-2 or N-1. The battery commander then ranges his gun for this last correction, and the shooting goes on until something else happens.

For instance, while I was controlling fire in this manner, all of a sudden my battery might cease firing. Not another shot would fall, and no more flashes would come from the gun pits. Looking around I would then be pretty certain to see a Heinie, as we call the German airmen, floating somewhere near me.

Of course that Heinie had come over to spot the battery which was molesting his own. The commander of my battery had seen him before I could and for that reason had ordered "cease fire," so that the location of the guns would not be given away. You can bet that if that Hun had spotted our guns and got the position down, that very night they would have been shelled.

One day a Hun plane came over the aerodrome after we had gone up and found it too misty to operate. We had hardly reached the ground again when out of that pea soup overhead came down in our own code the message:

"Too misty! Go home!" Only it was a Hun birdman who had given us that kind message. Yes, Mr. Hun is a very clever person on improvisations. Knowing that we relied on the smallest wireless sets we could get, he would erect a powerful wireless station somewhere behind his lines and then with the waves of that line he would obliterate the weak electrical impulses with which we worked. As a rule they would wait until about three or four machines were up and then they would jam them completely out of hearing. In this case those on the ground who were listening for our signals would hear nothing but the loud call of the powerful Hun station.

But Mr. Hun did even more than that. He knew our code of signals, and would wait

## BATTERING THE HUN

until a machine spotted a gun somewhere near a target, but not close enough for our observers to advise the use of the entire battery. Then he would come in with his call and order a salvo. The battery commander, not knowing that the signal was not from his own observer, would fire and, maybe, waste from ninety to one hundred rounds of good ammunition in an open field.

Meanwhile, the infuriated pilot or his observer would have to race back to the aerodrome and telephone to the battery to stop it.

Later, the target might be taken on again by means of a new code or through some other method of signalling, such as electric lamps. And thus the silent kill would go on.

It was not long before I discovered that the early morning and just before dusk were the best time for patrol work. I generally got more information then than at any other time of the day, for this time is especially well suited for observation behind the actual lines on account of morning and evening movements.

I always looked for the cookhouses of Fritz,

and I was aided in this by the fact that there was little wind which would allow the little wisps of smoke to rise well above the ground. My pilot would then get over the German lines, swoop down, and I would deposit a bomb among Fritz's "eats."

These bombs I would very often make myself the day before by ramming into a piece of pipe a charge of dynamite to give it a good punch. Into one end I would stick a bit of fuse and a detonator which was then lighted by means of a cigarette lighter.

These bombs proved regular surprise parties to Fritz, who would run like sin when one of them dropped near him. Very often he kept his eye too long on the machine instead of on his feet, and it was quite funny to see some of the tumbles he took. There were many other Fritzies who never got up again.

In the end I lost my love for bombing Huns at such close range. Once they put a bullet through our gasoline tank and we had just enough of it in our emergency tank to take us back to our lines in safety. The bullet came through a corner of the fussalage, went through the tank, and hit the nether side of my seat, which happened to be the top of the tank. Needless to say I jumped so high that my head hit the top plane. I had a horrible vision of being wounded in such a place. Just think of the monotony of standing up all the time while the cure is going on. But I found no trace of blood, and was correspondingly grateful. I had only been bruised enough to make me appreciate what a wound in that part of my anatomy would mean. While I was recovering from the shock, it occurred to me that it would be well to stop the leak in the tank with my finger. But by that time so little juice was left in it that it really was not worth while. On arriving home I fished the bullet out of the tank and I have saved it for a souvenir.

The experience did not entirely disgust me with these pleasant little excursions. But I was careful thereafter to supply my home-made bombs with longer fuses and drop them from a greater height.

Orders were received at headquarters one day that every man must make his will—a cheerful job. There was very little that I

## THE FLYING FIGHTER

had to bequeath to anyone but what there was I left to my mother. An Irishman named Holleran, who was full of Irish wit and as well read as he was witty, drew up his own will, and when he handed it to the commanding officer of the squadron, he said:

"Well, sir, I am a Socialist, and I believe in Socialism. I've got nothing, and I want to divide it with everybody."

Poor old John! He was the life of the squadron until he and his pilot were hit by one of our own shells and brought down in Hunland.

## CHAPTER XII

### "PIZZ" AND "RANDIE"

One of the most consistent combinations of pilot and good fellow was to be found in Phil Prothero. He was a daredevil Scotsman. He was wild; that is to say he would do anything in the world.

"Pizz," as we called him, flew a little scouting machine and spent the greater part of the time keeping the guns and sights on his machine in perfect order. He had brought down four Huns, but of late he had had a streak of bad luck. He would get up at three in the morning, go down to the 'drome, and have his machine pulled out of the hangar by the sleepy mechanics. Then he would pile into his flying clothes, get up about fifty feet from the ground, and come rushing over the camp, waking the rest of us up on his way to the lines in search of a Hun who might be doing an early patrol. But he never got his chance until he had lost many a good morning's sleep. One morning, after he had been doing this sort of thing for about two weeks, he happened to be a few miles behind the Hun lines and was flying low, since the ground mist made it hard to see from a great height.

"Pizz" was sailing along when he was suddenly surprised by the rat-a-tat-tat of the machine gun of a Hun who had settled on his tail. He sized the situation up in a flash, looped over the Hun and fired about ten shots, when his well petted gun jammed. "Pizz" simply went wild and had to drop out of the fight. There was nothing to do but return home for repairs.

He landed and had the jam rectified by the gunsmith of the squadron and away he went again to the lines, looking for his Hun.

But the Hun was no longer aloft, so "Pizz" went over to a German 'drome and there he found one who was just getting up into the air.

"Pizz" let him get up a ways and then fell upon him like a hawk, bringing him down on his own 'drome. "Pizz" then went very low over the German hangars and fired the rest of his ammunition at the frightened men, who ran all over the place looking for cover. After putting the fear of the Lord into the Huns on the aerodrome properly, "Pizz" started for home, climbing all the time to cross the lines at a good height. But the Hun Archies got a line on him and started to explode high explosive shrapnel all around him.

Just as he was crossing the lines homeward bound, a "woolly bear" burst right near him, knocking his engine out of the machine. The machine was completely unbalanced by this and now uncontrollable, but "Pizz" kept his head and got ready for the crash. It came all right and poor old "Pizz" was pretty badly damaged, having four ribs broken, his face cut and bruised, in addition to sustaining several internal injuries.

He went to the hospital for a while but soon recovered. He was sent to a famous fighting squadron and there he was just as wild as ever. He went up one day, and while on patrol tackled the Red Hun, so called because his machine was painted red. They fought for twenty-five minutes and finally poor old "Pizz" was shot down.

## THE FLYING FIGHTER

Another scout came along and soon the Red Hun was engaged in another battle. He was a good pilot and showed it by the way he played for position, darting hither and thither, but the Allied airman proved too much for him, and before long the Hun came down in a spinning nose dive and on fire. He came down so fast that one could hear the machine whistle as it came hurtling through space, then the sound of crashing wood and rending of fabric. And in two minutes nothing was left but a small heap of burning wreckage. So passed the Red Hun.

We all mourned old "Pizz," for every one liked him. We buried the remains of the Red Hun, for he had been a real sportsman. But there was little left of him. That little we gathered in a sack and the chaplain read the burial services at his grave.

We then sent a message by air to his aerodrome, telling of the fight and burial, and a short time later we received the same sort of message concerning "Pizz," and we all felt better.

But patrol work and artillery fire spotting, with now and then a long reconnaissance trip,

## "PIZZ" AND "RANDIE"

were not all of our tasks. We used to take photographs up in the air and found that quite interesting. These things made up our daily routine and it had to be some very exceptional thing in the end which at all impressed anybody. The exigencies of our calling were such that we grew not only indifferent to danger, but we became also very blasé towards everything. There was a great deal of keen rivalry, even to a fighting point, among the various squadrons, but what hard feeling there was generally vanished when some man died. In that case it was found that he had always been everybody's friend and his memory was held sacred by all.

Routine is likely to give life very commonplace aspects, as we thought, until some daredevil pilot would volplane us to the ground and add a few somersaults or loops just before he landed in the field, just to break the monotony. Some of the pilots had a habit of just missing the tops of our huts in order that the noise of the motor might break our sleep in the small hours of the morning. We might get up and curse the man until the air was blue and shout vengeful words after him, but that would do no good. The fact is that right down in your heart you loved that same fellow like a brother.

In the air service men will stand on the ground and shudder at sights that they themselves have been responsible for when over the lines of the enemy. Moreover, you always have a feeling for any of the boys who are doing their bit in the danger zone. And after that you get into your bus and go up and do more of it.

Even a pilot ofttimes stands on the ground and shivers to see some of the things another flyer is doing. But he will climb into his own machine and go up and do the same stunts himself.

But there were times when I had reason to wish myself back on the ground even if it was under the most terrific shell fire that I had seen. The man who is wounded in the trenches or out on the open field does not fall very far as a rule, and he has a fighting chance for his life. But the flyer who is hit in the air has a small chance, and it made me think of the old saying, "If you're hit on the

## "PIZZ" AND "RANDIE"

ground there you are, but if you're hit in the air where are you?"

However, I had joined the air service for better or for worse and I made up my mind to stick to it. I saw a lot of machines shot down in the course of time. Some of them took fire up in the air. Others crumbled to bits as they hit the ground, and in nearly all cases their crews were killed. Now and then the men in the machine would still live a day or two before they made their last trip West. But in only a few cases did men live long after they had come to earth from any great height in a machine which was out of control.

I used to think this thing over, but the thought never occurred to me that my end would come in that fashion.

I was summoned to appear before the commanding officer one day. He needed a gunner for a pilot who was going to take photographs. I felt less like flying on that day than I had ever done, but I went nevertheless—I went because I had no choice, of course. The commanding officer of a squadron is to the men of his unit a little god, whose word is law and whom you dare not disobey if you wish to avoid unpleasant consequences.

So when the officer said, "Roberts, you go with Hyatt as gunner," I said:

"Yes, sir."

That was all there was to it. I might have thought a lot, but those thoughts will always remain unspoken. For orders must be obeyed to the letter, whether the job is dangerous or not, under penalty of court martial for cowardice, so reads the little book called King's Rules and Regulations.

We got to a good height in very little time. In those days the average photograph was taken at the height of from 6,000 to 7,000 feet.

It happened to be a perfectly clear day in May. We got to the Hun lines and they were waiting for us it seemed. As soon as we stuck our noses over their lines they started to shell us for all they were worth. I had never seen such a shelling of an aeroplane before, and I confess that I was thoroughly frightened—almost frantic. The pilot was intent upon making good photographs, and he

## "PIZZ" AND "RANDIE"

had to stay within the 7,000 feet altitude in order to get them.

There being no Hun plane up, I had little to do. I was kneeling in my seat and looking for Huns but not a one came, nor was there any reason why they should in all that "Archie" exhibition. The chances were very good that the Hun anti-aircraft batteries would get us down without some Heinie having to take a risk. We circled and circled over the German lines until Hyatt had taken fifty-six photos, as fine a collection of the Hun first, second and third lines as had ever been made.

When Hyatt had done that he had to prolong the agony by photographing the Hun reserve positions; not that he wanted to, for he was as frightened as I was. And after that we concluded that we might just as well fly back home.

Well, when we counted the holes in our planes in the aerodrome we discovered that ninety-six holes, of various sizes, made by high explosive shrapnel, had robbed our planes of much of their carrying capacity. A few more and the old bus would have settled

## THE FLYING FIGHTER

down in Hunland no matter how much speed the motor might kick up.

I was interested in the course which some of the shrapnel balls had taken and discovered that many of them had come too close for solid comfort. One of them, for instance, must have missed my ankles by the veriest fraction of an inch. Another one had gone through the plane near the pilot and accounted for a slit nine inches long in Hyatt's leather coat.

I must make another remark about the holes in our planes. They were not small by any means. One of them was large enough for a cat to be thrown through. I guess that a whole shrapnel case must have gone through the plane. Shrapnel holes in the planes and the smaller perforations left by machine gun bullets had ceased to be of any consequence to the boys, however.

When I first entered the air service men still counted such things, and on the aerodromes they used to establish records based on the number of holes in a machine. But that got to be an old joke. The only performance which counted at this time was to

## "PIZZ" AND "RANDIE"

come hurtling through the air for several thousand feet, land on the nose of the machine, and then get from under the wreck with enough life left in you to make patching up worth while. If that could be done from ten to fifteen thousand feet, well and good, and if en route the gasoline tank took fire, good night. Nothing short of that could get a thrill out of the tough lot they had around the aerodromes.

We used to have considerable fun with the captive balloons of the Huns. The purpose of our attacks on them was to set them on fire, for nothing short of that could ever hurt them unless you shot them full of machine gun bullets. These captive balloons went up rather high, so our machines had a fair chance at them, if they could surprise them.

The bombs we used to drop on the captive balloons were of a deadly nature not only in so far that the phosphorus they contained would ignite the gas, but in addition to that they were deadly if dropped on the men in the trenches, as they produced incurable burns, and the fumes were horrible to breathe, as they contained a sort of gas. Old Randie, one of our pilots, was sent over one day to get a Hun sausage. He went up three times before he finally got it.

This particular sausage had had a great deal of our attention. It never came up twice in the same place, but moved up or down the road a hundred yards before it ascended. Generally, it was from two to three miles behind the lines.

We all wondered what this Hun was up to, and Randie was sent up to find out. With his load of bombs aboard he started up. The Hun watched him come, for to the Hun an Allied flying machine means death in various ways.

This one knew that Randie was after him, so he had his balloon pulled down as soon as Randie came at all near him.

But the Hun seemed very anxious to continue his observations and went up again. Randie, who had returned, started for him once more. In that manner they played hide and seek for about two hours.

Finally Randie climbed up and found a hiding place behind a cloud. The other thought that his tormentor was gone, but dis-

## "PIZZ" AND "RANDIE"

covered shortly that he was mistaken. When the balloon was up about half way, Randie took a dive from his hiding place and made straight for it, and then pulled the plugs to release the bombs. The two Huns in the captive balloon saw it coming, but there was nothing that they could do. Randie was upon them before they knew it, and as soon as the bombs hit they both jumped. It is not the prettiest sight in the world to see two men jump out of a balloon at four thousand feet from the ground.

The parachute of one of the men opened after a fall of five hundred feet or so. That stopped his rapid progress through the air and he descended safely enough. But the parachute of the other Hun never opened at all and he looked like a weighted rat as he sailed earthward. A speck of dust showed where he hit. He was only a Hun but he was game, and old Randie afterwards told me that he felt sorry for him. And Randie knew; he was an old timer, and game to the core.

Randie made the supreme sacrifice a short time later when he was hit by a high explosive shell while flying at about one thousand feet.

Randie was an Englishman—an English public schoolboy, well brought up. There is something in the training those boys get in one of those schools which they never forget. They are gentlemen and they show this quality. An Englishman who has been through Eton, Oxford or Harrow can be spotted as soon as you start talking to him, and he is generally as game as they make them. I have met several in my travels and they nearly all pan out alike.

And Randie was no exception to the rule. He was a gentleman and a sport. He did not believe in hard work, but he did believe in efficiency. He read a lot, and once in a while you would see Randie drop his book and call for his bus. The mechanics, who liked him as much as we did and who would do anything for him, would get his bus out. Then Randie would put on his helmet and fly out to the line just to tease the Huns, as he called it. He would fly behind the Hun lines and of course the "Archies" would start working on him, and for every shell that "Archie" exploded Randie would give him a loop.

## "PIZZ" AND "RANDIE"

Randie would do that for a time and then take a dive at the Hun lines, empty out two or three drums of ammunition, and fly back home. Then he would get out his book and start to read again just as if nothing had happened.

## CHAPTER XIII

### DAREDEVILS

IN the days when flying was largely defence and observation, and not on such a large scale as it is now, the pilots in various squadrons used to try and beat each other doing tricks or stunts with aeroplanes. One man would go up and do a series of loops, another did tail slides and stalls, as we term a manœuvre in which the machine is brought to a dead stop after reaching the apex of an upward curve. Another would do side slides and nose dives. And soon every one could do everyone else's stunts. Flying schools taught pupils that a spinning nose dive was fatal and no one had ever gotten out of one alive.

In 1916 some daredevil pilot flying a new type of machine, while flying along would roll his machine completely over sideways. Then some other pilot figured how to get out of a

## DAREDEVILS

spinning nose dive without injuring himself or the machine. Then the roll was applied while the machine was upside down at the top of a loop, which meant that the machine was started into a loop, and while upside down on the top of the loop it was rolled over to its proper position.

Soon the scout schools were teaching their pupils to do all such stunts, and they were applied to gain time or to win advantage over an adversary while engaged in combat, or to dodge anti-aircraft shells. In this manner the art of flying was developed by leaps and bounds.

It was surprising to see the number of evolutions a machine could be put through by a pilot who could do stunts properly. It was a common occurrence to see the machines come back from the lines and patrol work doing all kinds of funny stunts. They would cut all sorts of queer figures like a litter of playful kittens. There were a number of other stunts in which the pilots took pride, such as flying just a few feet from the ground behind the German lines, or skipping just over the tops of the parapets of the Hun front lines, using their machine guns as they went. These manœuvres were very dangerous, but a flying man in his prime never thinks of danger—if he did he would quit flying.

In the early part of 1916 I used to fly as observer for a daredevil pilot best known as K. K.'s one ambition was to touch the wheels of his under carriage on the ground somewhere behind the Hun lines.

Generally when a man does things that are forbidden something happens. Fate seems to punish one for the things that are foolhardy. And if fate had punished K on this special occasion I might not be here to tell the tale. But fortunately fate waited until our return to the aerodrome.

We were up on an early morning patrol, having started at dawn, and there was no action behind the German lines, as was usually the case at that hour in the morning. The sun was just starting to show itself over the horizon and with it came the promise of a fine day, which meant lots of work.

I was busy looking for a battery of German guns which had been reported active the night before, when all at once the Hun aircraft batteries opened fire on us. The explosion of the shells came so thick and heavy that our machine was tossed around by the concussion as if it were a cigarette paper. K shut off his power, and I kept watch to find the batteries that were doing the shooting. I found one on the way down, but I soon lost all eagerness to put it out of action, for K made no attempt at getting back to our lines.

I looked over to make sure he was not wounded, and, as the engine still turned, I wondered what was happening.

We went down behind the German lines until we were just over the tree tops. K then opened the throttle and the engine responded all right, but he closed it again, and I can't describe the strange sensation I had. I swallowed my heart, and made up my mind that I was to be a prisoner for the duration of the war.

That thought was not pleasant, especially after hearing the hair-raising tales which were told of the way our prisoners were being treated by the Germans. I shouted to K that the engine was all right, but he merely looked at me. I put a drum of ammunition on my Lewis gun, for I had made up my mind to kill him if he were a spy, and then I would make the attempt to fly the machine back myself.

We glided gently down and touched the ground. Over the field I saw three German soldiers racing to capture us. Just then K pulled open the throttle and away we went up in the air once more. My nerves just quivered with joy, and I took aim at our would-be captors and let the bullets fly in a stream. But the air currents near the ground were so erratic that I did not hit them. We headed for home.

As we crossed our own lines I heaved a sigh of relief. K looked at me and smiled. He had realized his ambition to touch the ground behind the German lines, but he had also given me the scare of my life, for I did not know what he was about. K swore me to secrecy as it meant an awful "strafing" if the squadron commander ever heard of his exploit.

I kept my word until poor K had touched the ground behind the German lines for the

## DAREDEVILS

last time. The commanding officer and I met in England one day and I told him all about it. He did not say much, but I could see that he was thinking very hard.

They have some beautiful summer days in France, especially in June and July, the months in which the Somme offensive began in 1916. I was up one day about three o'clock in the afternoon spotting fire for one of our batteries. I was at an elevation of six thousand five hundred feet and about six miles to the rear of the Hun lines.

I was keeping our lines in my sight, however, which is a proper habit with flying men. Of a sudden I noticed that it became difficult to see them; then I noticed that the sky was gradually being blotted out by heavy storm clouds which were coming from all directions.

I drew the pilot's attention to this. He was of the opinion that he would have to climb over the clouds. That sounded good to me. I did not want to return to the aerodrome just then for the reason that the Hun batteries, taking advantage of the storm, were giving it to our lines hot and heavy, and in doing so they were showing their locations by the flashes of the pieces.

I was taking down the location of the batteries on my map with the intention of having them later shot up by the 60-pounders of old Mac's battery.

But that storm hit us fair and square within a few minutes; and when its first gusts struck us I had the sensation that our machine was being tossed about like a cigarette paper.

It was a lucky thing that I had strapped myself in, for otherwise I would have been thrown out. We were in a cloud that was so dense that I could not see the propeller nor even the tips of the wings. I looked at the aneroid, but it showed nothing that I could make anything of. It had grown so dark that the instrument could no longer be read.

At first we were surrounded by an absolute silence, and then the storm broke loose. Before very long we seemed to find ourselves in a veritable hell of lightning and crashing.

We traveled for quite a distance in the dark with no means of knowing our elevation. I

## DAREDEVILS

began to fear that we might hit a church steeple or a house or something else on the ground. The rain was now falling heavily and added to our confusion and difficulty. To make matters worse it dissolved the dye on the edge of my goggles. The mixture got into my eyes, which began to smart terribly.

With the rain beating into my face it was more necessary than ever to keep on the goggles. However, the dye that was running over them irritated me, so that finally I concluded to protect my eyes with my hands. But the rain bit into them, and the parts of my face that were exposed, so viciously that I had to put the goggles on again.

The same thing had happened to the pilot, who was as thoroughly blinded as myself and had crouched into the cockpit to find some protection.

The chances of weathering that storm did not seem very good, and it occurred to me that I was about due to collect something this time from the Huns.

My conclusion was not far wrong. Peeping over the side of the body of the machine I saw the backs of some horses just underneath us, and in another moment or two we had landed on the crest of a little hill.

I did not know whether or not we were on our own side of the line, but my mind was soon set at ease, for a British Padre came toiling up the hill and the first question he asked was if we had seen any captive balloons drifting about.

It seemed that three of our balloons had broken away. I hadn't seen any balloons nor had the pilot. After that we took time to thank our stars that we were still alive and had not landed a few miles further east in Hunland.

The battery commander, with whom we were doing the "shoot," had telephoned to the commanding officer of our squadron and had told him that we had last been seen going backward over the Hun lines. The good man was sure that he had seen us for the last time, and he was not a little surprised when we showed up.

It was some time before we could get in touch with the squadron, and when we did it we were just able to prevent our names from being put on the list of the missing. There

## DAREDEVILS

was a great reunion on our arrival at the squadron and we celebrated it that night in good old style by having wine with our supper.

Shortly after that I went out for patrol practice behind our own lines with a brigade of infantry who were to take part in the Somme offensive. The brigade in question had never been in action before, and since it was to have that chance in the near future it had to go through the necessary manœuvres.

After practicing for two hours I came down at the aerodrome and was told by the commanding officer that the general commanding the brigade was so pleased with my work that I was to have dinner with him.

I started for his headquarters in the afternoon and we discussed contact control and its merits while dining. After that he invited me to go with his staff on a big hunt in the near-by woods, where I was told still lived some wild boars.

That hunt proved to be a very interesting experience. Instead of guns long spears were used, and we rode the best horses that could be found. But I am not used to the flat sad-

## THE FLYING FIGHTER

dle and that was where my troubles began. I can ride almost any horse with a Mexican saddle, but to ride an English saddle, known in the Western States as a postage stamp, is a different thing. Nor was this all. The horse I was to ride was a fine hunter of good height who had been trained for fox hunting and he delighted in nothing so much as in taking every fence and hedge he came to. That spear, too, was in the way. It was about ten feet long and to me was a new implement. So between the spear and that horse, not to mention the saddle I was kept busy staying right side up.

The hunt had started in the forest and as we came to its edge we could hear the beaters shout. They were coming towards us and were driving a tusker before them. The animal came tearing through the underbrush. The first three hunters missed it and then the boar made straight for my horse. Had I been anything of a pig hunter at all I might have gotten him. But that was not to be. Just as the animal charged through the legs of my horse, he snarled viciously, and that hunter of mine, used more to foxes than to

## DAREDEVILS

boars, started off. That ended the pig hunt so far as I was concerned. For the next half hour we jumped fences and hedges in good style, and then we, or rather the horse, had had enough of it. I slipped off of the saddle, very sore in certain parts of my anatomy, and then walked the hunter back to headquarters, where I exchanged him for my more comfortable motor cycle and side car. And the general had a hearty laugh when I related to him my experience.

I drove back to headquarters a very sore man physically, but I found solace in the fact that in another five days my leave was due.

I was looking forward to the time I was to spend in England with a great deal of joyful anticipation, and I had enough money saved up to have another go at London.

The boys tried to kid me that night by saying:

"Oh, you will never see Blighty. What will you take for your turn on the leave-roster?"

The Somme offensive was to take place at any time now, and it was extremely hard for anybody to get leave. The chances of getting

## THE FLYING FIGHTER

away from the front for a little while, as I had promised myself, seemed indeed scant. That Somme offensive might last from a week to a year for all we knew. That was true enough, and the boys made it worse by dwelling on the fact that before it was over I would never need another leave. One of them suggested that I decide upon the sort of flowers I wanted the boys to bring to my funeral.

Imagine my disappointment, if you can. For weeks and weeks I had counted upon that trip to England, and now the Somme offensive was to shatter all my plans. But there was no help for it.

## CHAPTER XIV

### THE BIG PUSH

For the last three days before the offensive the contact patrol men were not allowed to fly. There was a great deal of tension noticeable everywhere, and to get away from that we sought some diversion in our surroundings.

I went to a little French village about two miles away just to look around and talk to the natives. I found them immensely interesting and they enlightened me on many points. I inquired among other things what their sports were and in what way they enjoyed themselves. I was surprised when the old veteran of former wars, with whom I was talking, went out and brought in a bow and a quiver full of arrows.

Now, archery is an odd form of sport, though very similar to trap shooting. I had seen the Indians out on the reservations in

## THE FLYING FIGHTER

Canada and in the States use bows and arrows, but not to a great extent, merely using them to amuse the children. But here it was considered almost a national sport. The old man explained how they held tournaments and even went to the extent of building tall lattice work masts, on the tops of which the birds were arranged. Each competitor paid so much to participate in the shooting and the receipts were given out in prizes for the birds that were brought down.

The masts or perches are as much as one hundred and twenty-five feet high, and on the top of them is placed the master bird, for which the biggest prize is given. The other targets all have a value commensurate with the difficulty in hitting them.

The old man took me out in the hop field behind the house and showed me how to shoot. I must say that he was a master at it. One of the things he hit was a jam tin at fifty yards. I tried it a good many times, but that jam tin might as well have been a mile away. I visited the old man quite often and many a bow and arrow shoot we had together.

Shooting with a bow was not his only ex-

## THE BIG PUSH

ploit. He had been an old soldier and had fought in the war of 1870 and had many interesting tales to tell of how wars were fought before the aeroplane came into use. But he used to think it a miracle that a machine could stay up in the air at all. My efforts to make him understand why it could stay up were all Dutch to him. And as my French was not complete enough to tell him the difference between a strut and a camber rib I had to let the old man go on thinking that the good Lord or the devil had a lot to do with it. I once offered to take him up, but he looked at me and shook his old white head and replied:

"Non, mon cher ami! I am what you call ze scare for ze machine to fall on ze groun' an' I'm broke ma por ol neck. I thank you ze same like I go up wit' you."

While at another village one day I was informed that a great cock fight was to be held on the following Sunday.

To me that was something new. I inquired what the entrance fees were to be and I was told everything was free and that experts on the game would give me good tips on which birds to bet in case I wanted to make money.

## THE FLYING FIGHTER

I thought that there would be a good chance to get even with that gang of gamblers at the squadron, who had recently trimmed me quite a bit. I inquired about one of these tipsters, and I was introduced to a man who said he knew everything about cock fighting and every battling fowl in the country.

I made arrangements with him to tip me to the winners, for which I was to pay him twenty francs. We arranged to have the fights close to the squadron so that we could be handy to go up in the air at a minute's notice, as nothing was allowed to interfere with our work. Then I went home all worked up at the prospect of such an afternoon's sport and broke the news to the bunch, but I did not tell them of my plan to be the bookmaker of the event.

It would have to take place in the afternoon, as the people went to church in the morning.

We waited all the rest of the week and I had figured it all out how I was going to trim the boys on the bets. Sunday afternoon finally came on and the sportsmen gathered from far and wide with their game cocks in sacks.

# THE BIG PUSH

The arena, which had been erected, was made of canvas in the form of a little fence about two feet high. A canvas floor had been pegged down and it looked just like a prize ring.

The announcer got upon a chair and announced the first event, which was a sort of preliminary. About twenty of the boys had gathered around. I had made a little booking stall and, with my tipster as guide, I was to receive all comers in bets up to one hundred francs. He showed me the winner and the bout started.

Now these cocks were spurred according to the judgment of the owner and they had sure made a good job of it. The supposed winner had been armed with steel spurs two and one-half inches long. But the foolish bird was too eager and jumped at the other cock with no judgment, tripped himself, and went to the mat. The other cock climbed onto him and would have made a finish of him had he not been pulled off in time.

Betting had been active and my pile went down one hundred and fifty francs.

The next fight started and the tipster told

## THE FLYING FIGHTER

me that the winner would be the smaller cock of the two. His opponent was about twice his size, and I thought that if he did as much as fall on the little fellow he would surely kill him. But the tipster was supposed to know, and I took his word for it.

Well, the fight had no more than started than it was over. The big fellow just took one swipe at the little bird and ran one of his spurs through his neck.

The birds were taken out and the pile went down another one hundred and fifty francs.

There were only five more fights to take place, so I decided to discharge my tipster, having come to the conclusion that I knew as much about it as he did. The next two birds were quite evenly matched and I picked my own winner. He was a ragged looking bird, but he looked tough enough to bet on, so I took all comers against him. The betting was brisk and had I lost that fight I would have been cleaned out. But my bird won and I took in about two hundred francs.

On the fourth fight I lost one hundred francs, and just as the last fight was coming on I figured how much I would have to make

## THE BIG PUSH

to break even, when an orderly rushed over with orders for me to be on line patrol in five minutes.

I quit the fight about three hundred francs loser.

That cured me of betting on cock fights. The money did not matter much for one never knew but what he would be "gone West" any minute, and the only good use we had for money was to spend it on leave and pay mess bills. What was left over changed hands freely at roulette, or crown and anchor, and poker. The games were not big and no one lost heavily, but it sure helped to pass many a weary hour.

The big drive started, and for five days and nights it seemed that every gun on both sides had been brought down to the front on which we worked, and we soon found that a great many had. Drum fire and the like was known to us already, but a bombardment of the intensity such as ushered in the great infantry attacks was something entirely new to us.

The shelling done by both sides was terrific and we, who were able to watch it from the air, wondered how a single human being could survive the shock. For the time being nothing seemed to matter because everybody felt that a titanic struggle was on—a struggle which, it was hoped, would put an end to the war. The boys had started a tennis court near the aerodrome but all work on it ceased.

Our artillery did its best to break down the Hun lines and the Huns replied almost shot for shot. The earth shook day and night, and seven miles behind the windows rattled.

Into the trenches were being hurried thousands and thousands of men who were to follow up the advantages gained by the artillery.

The front had been a busy place the year before but now it was busier than ever. There was no end to the artillery ammunition convoys, and I used to wonder where Great Britain and France were getting all the men that they were hurrying to the front. Even cavalry, of which we had seen very little in the past, put in an appearance.

It rained in torrents for several days and that made aerial observation very difficult if not wholly impossible, besides making life a torture to the thousands of troops who had

## THE BIG PUSH

to live outside during the whole period. But one never heard a murmur of dissatisfaction.

On July 1st, at 4.30 in the morning, two planes from our squadron were ordered to proceed to the front for the purpose of doing contact patrol duty. We had three men in our squadron who were versed in that accomplishment. One of the men was named Davis, the other Sutton; I was the third. Sutton was to act as relief.

Davis and I had to keep over the trenches at an elevation of about two hundred feet, the weather being so bad that we had to fly low. We had to take messages from the men in khaki on the ground, following them as in one wave after another they advanced against the Huns. But they never got at the Huns. Though the barbed wire entanglements of the enemy had been cut in everywhere, it had been cleverly replaced by the Hun engineers. In a few places our men did get through, however, and it seemed that there the victory was to be ours.

Our work was not satisfactory, however. We could see very little of the fight for the reason that we had to cover much space and were hardly ever able to follow an operation to its conclusion. It was also impossible to gain much of an impression on the general situation. And generally we knew little of the progress that had been made until we returned to camp. The commanding officer of the squadron was not satisfied with our work. He complained that our message bags were going all over the country and he also had fault to find concerning an unfinished message which I had sent to headquarters by wireless. I was in the act of sending the message when my aerial was shot away, cutting my message in half. I dropped part of the message I had sent there and then, and it was picked up at headquarters. The other half of the message which I sent had not been received, as I had lost my aerial.

Knowing that the second half of the message was of great importance, the pilot and myself risked our lives by a dive down to within fifty feet of the ground so that we might drop a message bag at a station which was in a garden quite well enclosed by trees. As the machine rose again it came within a few inches of running into a balloon cable

## THE BIG PUSH

which we had not noticed. The cable was so thin that it was almost invisible until we were a few feet away from it. Nevertheless, we were reprimanded for running needless risks.

The officers along the Somme front were in no pleasant humor in those days. It was impossible to get a civil word from any of them, and everybody seemed bent upon taking it out on the other fellow. Everybody was being overworked and the strain, together with the anxiety as to what the result would be of this offensive, began to affect the disposition of everybody. So many preparations had been made for the work in hand and so much seemed to depend upon its successful conclusion that officers and men alike thought of nothing but the engagements that were going on. The slightest mistake on the part of anybody was usually magnified many times, until the culprit was sure that he was a criminal.

The Huns meanwhile were bringing down a good many Allied aviators. Two of the best men of our squadron were killed. One of them, "Little" Jowett, the smaller of two brothers of that name and a chap whom everybody liked very much, was shot down by the Huns while taking photographs behind their line. Poor old Stoddard was hit by a Hun machine gun from the ground, and he and his observer were killed in the crash. These were things that caused us to think hard, and many of us lost our care-free ways and began to wonder when it would be our turn.

One day I went up in the afternoon and did some very hard work. Some of our troops had managed to get into parts of Hunland and had to be carefully covered there. It was even harder out there to get messages into the proper hands. Knowing what it was to be in the trenches with the infantry, and feeling that Tommy Atkins needed all the assistance I could give him, I set about my duties with a will.

I realized how important it was to get my messages to headquarters where they could be acted upon. It was often a question of saving many lives. That kept my nerves high-strung during the four hours that I was on patrol. I was in the habit of putting my pencil in my mouth while using the wireless

## THE BIG PUSH

key, and discovered this afternoon that I had chewed it completely to bits.

At about four o'clock that afternoon I got a message from some of our men who were tied up in a small section of German trench and were being shelled there in addition to being machine gunned. They were in so tight a fix that they could go neither forward nor backward, while the Germans were swarming around them like bees around a hive. The message I picked up from the ground said that they were being held in by machine gun fire.

I could see that a Hun gun emplacement with six guns, all working at the same time, was causing the isolated group underneath me as much trouble as machine guns possibly could. So I sent a message to headquarters with a map reference of the location of the German guns and waited for developments.

I was soon rewarded with a sight which I shall never forget. Within five minutes of the time that I had flashed back my message, one of our batteries was putting into the German emplacement shells that hit the very spot. Next morning I had a good look at the place

## THE FLYING FIGHTER

but found nothing but a lot of shell holes and a few lifeless gray forms on the ground.

That day again we worked until darkness made it impossible to pick up messages from the ground. But even after that the fighting continued. The heavy detonations of the large guns and the explosion of the big shells kept up a fearful racket. As I soared aloft it seemed to me that all the world had gone crazy. The very air trembled and as far as the eye could reach was seen the flash of gun and shell. The powder fumes kept drifting over the ground. They were first illumined by the rays of the setting sun and later by the star shells. The scene was most spectacular.

Meanwhile the ambulances were rushing back and forth from advanced position to the field dressing stations, and later others took up the work clearing these stations by taking the wounded men to the rear. That work continued all night, and it was only then that we began to realize the heavy sacrifices that were being made by the men who went over the top.

That sort of thing went on for days and

## THE BIG PUSH

nights without interruption. It seemed to us that the work was piling up faster than we could attend to it. There was no limit to what the officers in charge demanded of their subalterns and men, and every nerve was being strained to the utmost. In the past I had gone up only occasionally, as it now seemed to me. But now I was up in the air almost constantly. My machine would hardly land before some orderly would pounce upon us with new instructions. We had barely time enough to eat in peace, and usually our sleep was interrupted at dawn, and very often before that. Few of us succeeded in ever getting our clothes off our backs. It was a case of work, work, work, and generally the devotion one tried to throw into this found little appreciation. At first some of us resented this, but finally we came to realize that the strain of responsibility upon the higher officers was such that nothing else could be expected from them.

I found myself at dawn one morning looking for a Hun battery which had been doing good work on some of our guns. It was foggy and so I was obliged to stay close to the ground, but I managed to get across the Hun advance positions without trouble and soon ran into their "Archie" batteries. That caused my pilot to go up. The fog between ourselves and the ground made observation almost impossible, but as good luck would have it I finally located the battery that had done the damage. I communicated with one of our batteries, which had the location of the enemy battery, and within a few minutes the Hun had stopped firing. I returned to our aerodrome after that, but was immediately sent off again to do contact control with some infantry organizations that were about to advance. I worked at this until 10:30 in the morning and then returned to the squadron. After an hour or so I started on volunteer reconnaissance. We were to find some of our infantry who had gotten into the Hun lines and had not been heard from since. The men had been lost on the preceding day and it was a question whether they could still be succored. I took many a risk scouting up and down the sectors in which the men in question had been lost, and finally was lucky enough to find them.

## THE BIG PUSH

Upon my return I was sent on patrol duty, looking this time for a German machine gun emplacement which had made itself very much disliked. But to find a well-screened machine gun position is not so easy. I had considerable trouble seeing anything from the elevation I was flying at and finally descended to about seventy-five feet. Meanwhile, my plane had attracted the attention of the Huns and their shells were bursting all around me. It was very difficult under these conditions to observe anything, but I had an idea where the machine guns were located. I went over the ground a good many times, but seemed unable to get the exact position. My patrol period came to an end before I had found the machine guns, but my relief, to whom I gave whatever information I had gathered, discovered that the guns had been placed in the cellar of a building that had been razed by artillery fire. The information was flashed back to a battery, and within a very little time that Hun machine gun emplacement was no more.

When the position had been silenced, the observer took a photograph of the scene and upon examination it was found that eight machine guns had been hidden in the cellar. Since each of these guns could fire as many as six hundred shots a minute and do terrible havoc, the haul had been a good one.

At 3:30 that afternoon I had another assignment—contact patrol with the infantry. Everything at that front was in such a turmoil with shell fire and smoke that I was able to see but few features of the ground. All buildings, and in some cases whole woods, had completely disappeared, so that the aerial observers were now obliged to find a new set of landmarks. The buildings and trees which in the past had served as valuable marks to us were gone. We began to realize that in future we would have to be guided by the things which heavy artillery could not carry off—the hills, for instance.

While on contact patrol I took messages until seven o'clock that night, when I was relieved by another machine. I returned to the aerodrome, made a general report and then tried to eat dinner, but the excitement of the battle had left my nerves in such a condition that I could not swallow a morsel.

## THE BIG PUSH

At 8:30 I was given an order to make a reconnaissance flight over Hunland. This time I went up with the commanding officer as pilot. We flew over the Hun lines at a very low altitude and approached a little village just back of the German positions. Near the village a relief party of Huns was just entering the communication trenches. We were so low that I could take them under fire with the machine gun, and I killed about thirty.

We then started towards the place for which we were bound in quest of the desired information. The trip was quite successful and before long we were sailing over No Man's Land on our return. But we were not home yet. Of a sudden I had the sensation of having been hit on the head with a hammer. For a moment I lost consciousness, but seemed to regain my senses immediately.

When I was again in control of myself, I noticed that the engine had stopped. I believe it was that fact which caused me to become conscious again. I looked around at my pilot and saw that his face was covered with blood and that blood had also run over his goggles.

## THE FLYING FIGHTER

My first thought was that he had been hit, and though he was sitting upright in his seat and seemed all right, I made frantic signs to him to start the engine. This he did, for a moment later the propeller began to spin. I fell back into my seat and once more lost consciousness.

When next I regained my senses I noticed that we were flying at a great height. My eyes fell upon a large wood which I recognized as one lying immediately behind our lines. I was still wondering why the pilot's face and goggles were covered with blood and was making an effort to slide back to him to find out what the matter was when he motioned me not to stir and stopped the engine, starting immediately gliding gently towards the ground.

"I'll take you down," said the pilot.

We had another place to go to and though I was feeling very badly, I thought we might be able to finish the job.

"No, go on," I said.

The pilot did not reply. Instead, he held the nose of the machine towards the ground.

Soon it became apparent that the pilot had

## THE BIG PUSH

reconsidered, for I noticed that we were swinging back over Hunland. As we neared the ground I saw that some of our men were engaged in consolidating parts of a position they had taken from the Huns.

The men in the trenches waved their helmets at us, and just then a volley of Hun bullets came up through the planes, making a noise like a snare drum as they spilt the canvas. After that we headed for general headquaters where, after making my report, I once more relapsed into unconsciousness.

When next I was conscious I found myself in the field dressing station. They were bandaging up my head, and somebody told me that my skull had been fractured by a bullet. I was then given the anti-tetanus treatment and five days later I was an inmate of a hospital on the French coast, the institution in question being presided over by the Duchess of Westminster.

I was operated upon twice and each time pieces of bone had to be removed. I was unconscious the greater part of the time. One morning I awoke in another place and learned upon inquiry that I was in a hospital in England and that within a few days I would have to undergo another operation.

The next time I came to my senses I had been operated upon, but found that I could neither hear, see, nor talk. I was very weak, and seemed unable to think rationally. The slightest effort I made at reasoning caused some of the factors which I wished to bring into relation with one another to recede from my grasp. With my senses of sight and hearing gone, I had to rely entirely upon my sense of touch. I could feel the nurses doing things around my bed, but aside from that no external impressions came to me. I tried to make them understand what I wanted, but such efforts were unavailing. I supposed nobody could understand the feeble movements of my hands. Though the care that was given me seemed to be a matter of routine, it was, nevertheless, ample.

For two weeks that continued. My bed had meanwhile been placed against the wall in a ward known as the Turner Ward. I felt that windows and doors had been opened for the purpose of airing the room. Suddenly a door near me was shut with a bang. I did not hear that bang, of course, but I felt the vibrations of it, which caused me to jump, and as I did this I saw of a sudden two rows of beds on either side of the room. A nurse was coming towards me.

The same instant my powers of speech returned.

As I looked at the nurse the thought came to me that possibly I was mistaken in all this. I had groped about in the darkness so long that I was now doubting the very things I beheld.

"Are you wearing a white apron and a blue dress?" I asked the nurse.

Instead of answering my question, the woman ran off, and I heard her call a doctor.

Within thirty minutes I was once more on the operating table.

When the effect of the anesthetics left me, I was indeed grateful to discover that the senses which had deserted me for a while were still with me. I could see, hear and talk. These functions were still impaired, I discovered, and for a while I was tortured by the thought that again I might lapse into my former helpless position. Gradually, however, I managed to get them under better control, and before long I felt that my physical vigor was also returning.

While at the hospital, I learned a great deal of our old squadron. Its men had not fared well. "Little" Jowett, I learned, had been accompanied by a corporal gunner when their machine was brought down by the Huns. The gunner had been taken prisoner.

Jimmie, a Canadian chap, had been wounded and it was believed that he would be permanently crippled. Randie had been killed. Old John and his pilot, Captain Burney, two of the best men living, had gone down. "Fat" Brennan, another Canadian, had been wounded. Davis had suffered shell shock and Bolitho had been killed. Six members of the original squad were still alive; all the others had been taken on their last flight. I also heard that the squadron commander, one of the best in the world, had been promoted to be a wing commander.

There is no doubt that war is exactly what Sherman said it was. You see a pal one day

## THE BIG PUSH

and the next day he is either dead or missing. But often they made mistakes in the casualty list. Once for ten months I was left under the impression that a good friend of mine had been killed. Really he had been taken prisoner by the Huns. I met him in a hotel in London, and had some trouble making sure that he was really the man I knew. The same thing happened to me. My name appeared on the casualty list among the missing several times. Then when I would show up at some aerodrome everybody would wonder why I wasn't dead. The worst of it was that my old mother received cables of my being wounded or killed on five different occasions. The trouble in my instance was that in so big a crowd as an army almost any given name is found a good many times; and then generally somebody has the knack of thinking that the particular Smith or Jones who has been killed is the one he knew. There were times when it was indeed difficult to keep track of one's friends because the casualty lists were so large.

I received the best of care in the English hospitals and in two weeks after my last operation I was able to walk around quite well. After that I started in search of my baggage, which had not been delivered to me. Before long I found what was left of it. The thing that hurt me most was that all my good Hun souvenirs had been taken, and I was never able to trace one of them.

# CHAPTER XV

### LEARNING TO FLY

Upon my discharge from the hospital, I reported to the general in charge in England, and he, after reading the report of my case, advised me not to fly any more. It took considerable pleading on my part to induce the officer to retain me in the service. But after a heart-to-heart talk, I induced him to let me remain in the Flying Service. For the time being I was to be sent to a school of instruction, where I was to be initiated in the art of operating a machine myself. The course I was to take included the theories of aviation, construction of machine, flight rigging, operation, and general flying and mechanics as applied to air motors. To this was added meteorology and physics, bombing, and such things as wire splicing and the other little odds and ends one has to know in order to keep an airplane in good trim.

## THE FLYING FIGHTER

I passed the examination easily enough.

Having had some experience in actual flying and fighting at the front, I was later required to do some lecturing in different classes. Though I had never lectured before and had some difficulty addressing a class, I soon managed to gain some proficiency in this. My lectures covered the work I had done in France, such as observation for artillery, contact patrol, and aerial fighting. There was no school of aerial gunnery on the training ground in question, and for that reason my lectures interested the students very much.

I found that many of the men at the school were of my turn of mind when I was in Canada. Every one of them wanted to get to the front and fight, and gave little thought to the fact that before a man can fight he must be instructed and trained. Coming in contact with this tendency as an instructor I now began to realize what a trial I must have been in my recruit days.

We had a Scotchman at the school who was of the regular daredevil variety. Discipline meant absolutely nothing to him. There was

## LEARNING TO FLY

no order that he would obey and the result of it was that his troubles never ended.

We had been quartered in an old English Hall. The buildings, laid out on the lines of a U, had been erected many centuries ago, I was told, and the lawn in the yard was looked upon as something highly venerable for the reason that it had been planted by the original owner of the place. The recruits, who were a rather tough lot, had acquired the habit of using that lawn as a playground. To this the present owner objected, with the result that the commanding officer had a sign put up prohibiting trespass on the lawn under a penalty of five shillings for each offense.

McCray, the Scotchman in question, was in the habit of rushing across this lawn whenever he wished to reach the dining-room. He had done this one morning at breakfast. The commanding officer saw him, administered a stinging reprimand, and wanted to collect the fine. McCray reached into his pockets and finding that he had nothing smaller than a ten-shilling note gave it to the commanding officer with the words:

"Here's ten bob! Take it all and I'll walk

across it once more after I've had ma' breakfast, as I don't want to be late for the first class, sir."

The commanding officer warned him, but McCray walked across the lawn all the same. There is no doubt that the lot of the officer training recruits is not the easiest one can imagine.

After passing my examination, I was sent back to France to learn practical flying with the Royal Naval Air Service Squadron. I was gratified to find that it did not take me long before I could handle a machine. I had gained considerable experience in flying as an observer. The machines we had used at the front had a double set of controls, so that observers were able to get their hand in gradually. These machines also were fitted with machine guns that did not synchronize with the propeller, and although the observer had to do most of the fighting, there were times when the pilot had to operate the wireless. In this case the observer was entrusted with steering the plane.

I learned how to fly on a Cauldron, a French type of machine with a radial engine of 100

## LEARNING TO FLY

H.P. and a warp control. After an hour's flight with an instructor, I made my first solo flight—that is, I went up alone. I found that I had little trouble handling the machine, and made a good landing.

On my second flight I tried my best to break the squadron's altitude record, which was then 11,000 feet. I was up for nearly two hours, and reached an elevation of 10,500 feet—when "bang!" went the revolution counter.

That did not worry me, however. The engine showed no sign of having been impaired and kept on running. I decided to climb some more.

I was quite a ways above the clouds, in the eternal blue, when all of a sudden the engine stopped. Well, that made a lot of difference. There are no places in the air to which one can throw an anchor, so there was nothing that could prevent my coming down suddenly.

I tried to locate the trouble, but found that keeping the machine on an even keel would occupy me entirely without giving any attention to the motor. I began to dive. It so happens that a Cauldron has no gliding angle. It glides as gently as a brick.

It did not take me long to fall through the clouds, which, as I had observed going up, were then about 4,000 feet above the ground. I was through that bed of dense and damp mists before I knew what had happened, but I had sense enough to keep my eyes open for the aerodrome or some other convenient spot on which to land.

Just how I would land worried me considerably. I wanted to do as little damage as possible. There were hundreds of machines in this aerodrome. Many of them would be standing about the ground and others might be on the wing.

Fortunately, no machines came into my path. I took a curve to one side of the aerodrome and made ready for the long glide that was to get me to the ground. I was nearing the ground at a great speed when I noticed the "skipper" waving his arms like a madman. I thought that he wanted me to steer away from some machine near me and in my haste to obey his orders I turned right towards the officer. That caused him to cease

## LEARNING TO FLY

shouting and waving his arms. He started to run across the aerodrome as fast as anybody ever did run, with me and my faithful chariot just two steps behind him. The way that skipper covered territory was a sight to behold. Well, the machine lost its momentum and then the commanding officer risked coming near us.

He seemed speechless. All he could do was to shake a wrathful fist at me. He was red in the face. But presently speech came to him, and then I heard what he thought of me. That good man called me every name in the calendar and a few others that are generally included in the category known as From Hell to Breakfast. He did all this without using any punctuation. The skipper was an old salt and knew exactly how to do it.

He left me with the remark that I would be under arrest for two weeks—as I was. But that did not bother me any. All life at the front and behind the front was like being in jail anyway. We had come to the point where we could visit the girls no longer and even in the guardhouse one might shake poker dice, the only recreation that was now left to us.

But playing poker with French cards is not so simple. The Kings and Jacks looked very much alike and are identified only by the initials of their French proper nouns. For that reason we took to dice. I was not the only one in that guardhouse. There was a Canadian chap named Cameron. He was as good-hearted as they make them. Cam, as we called him for short, did not know the value of money at all and certainly loved to gamble.

The two weeks under arrest passed quickly enough and then our training was continued. Cam and I started out one morning to do solo work. The weather was rather muggy so that we could not be seen from the ground after we had gone up a short distance. We made up our mind to have a little vacation that day. When we were quite sure that the skipper could not tell where we were, we sailed to a little French town about twenty miles away. We knew that there was landing ground near by, and for that reason we could risk it.

## LEARNING TO FLY

We landed all right but began to doubt if the weather would stay what it was. If it cleared up that skipper would look for us up in the blue welkin, and then there would be trouble. But we had some money in our pockets and wanted to eat a regular dinner. To get that we had to go down the main street of the town to find a restaurant.

After much hunting we found one. We must have been the first English officers that ever ate in the place, to judge by the conduct of the proprietor and his waitress. The girl made it her business to pull back the curtains at the window so that the people passing by could see the distinguished patrons of the restaurant. The meal they served us was good. To show that we had a little money in our pockets, Cam and I picked up two ragged little girls and took them to a store where we dressed them up from shoes to hat. That made quite a sensation. The idea was Cam's, and he was certainly pleased with himself that it had been carried out.

We were lucky that the weather had remained hazy. We got into our machines and made off, but took great care that on ap-

## THE FLYING FIGHTER

proaching our aerodrome we were well out of sight. The skipper was waiting for us on the ground and seemed quite pleased that we were such good students.

Well, poor old Cam did not last so very much longer. He went to the front, and before he left he told me that he had a feeling that he would never get back. I tried my best to get that notion out of his head but did not succeed. A little while later I saw his name in the casualty lists under: Killed in Action. How the Huns got him in the air I never found out. He had been over the top on many occasions with the Canadians in the north of France and had never been touched, and he had proved to be a very skilful pilot.

Cameron, by the way, had the habit of calling the French "puddle jumpers," on account of their excitability. At mess one day the skipper asked him why it was that the average Frenchman became excited so easily.

Cameron had considerable Irish wit.

"Well, sir," he said, "they all love their Paris, and no doubt it is a wonderful city, and I guess there is not a Frenchman in

## LEARNING TO FLY

France who has not seen Paris. They get their excitement from dodging taxicabs in Paris, and as there are a lot of puddles in the streets of Paris, hence the name of 'puddle jumpers,' which I have given them.''

The Cauldron machine in which I continued to fly got on my nerves after a while. It was very hard to make good landings with it. One day the skipper told me that I was to land as close to the sheds as possible. I said that I would do so, and, after having had a good "flip" up in the air, I came down with the skipper's instructions still in mind. He was watching me. I was going to make a particularly good landing. When the wheels of the bus hit the ground for the first time, a hard bump came of it, and the fine plan I had made was thrown out of gear. Close by the place where I had intended to land stood another machine. The bump had somewhat changed the direction of my plane, and since I was still going at a speed of about thirty miles an hour I feared that I would crash into the other machine.

There was only one way of preventing that; I would have to go up again. I pulled the throttle of the motor to a ninety-mile clip, to the great astonishment of the skipper, who had fully made up his mind, it seems, that I was going to break up everything. He grew wildly excited, but I did not mind him. Instead I opened the throttle some more and then "zoomed" over the machine and the shed beyond.

I was still "zooming" when I saw the trees behind the shed; they were about three times as high as the shed itself. It was a case of either getting over or crashing into them. To get over the trees I thought impossible. There is no machine that would rise that much in the short distance that lay between my machine and the tree tops.

The only thing to do to avoid a very bad spill was to have more speed. I opened the throttle still more, with the result that the machine began to want to dive. To overcome that I pulled her nose up, increased my speed again and pulled into the final "zoom."

As I did this I got a glance of the skipper and several of the instructors, who were rushing around, wildly watching what I was doing. I just got over the tree tops by a hair.

## LEARNING TO FLY

Of course it was as good as a mile, but very dangerous. After all, a Hun is a Hun and always does funny things. Right then and there I promised myself a month in the guardhouse, and the thought put a rather peculiar notion into my head. If I had to go to the guardhouse for a month I wanted to give them good cause for it.

Near the aerodrome was a railroad track and just then a train was coming along it. It was against all rules and regulations to chase trains or dive at engine drivers. But I went after this one and put the wind of my propeller down the back of his neck. After that I raised Cain with some cattle in a field nearby and then I started back for the aerodrome.

The skipper had been waiting for me. It was getting dark and I was the only man who had been up and who had not returned. This time my landing was more successful. It was a landing of the sort the skipper liked.

I rolled right up to the shed, switched off, and climbed out. I stood at attention ready to take my medicine.

## THE FLYING FIGHTER

But I nearly dropped in my tracks when the skipper began to speak.

"My boy," he began, "you had us all frightened to death. We thought you would never get over those trees. You made the record 'zoom,' but our hearts were up in our throats all the time. It was a great piece of flying, but for God's sake don't ever do it again. You will report in the morning at my office."

I spent a very uncomfortable night, being constantly plagued by speculation as to what the skipper wanted me for.

Though the old man had given no sign of being angry, I feared that he had calmed down while I was chasing the train and the cows, but had not forgotten.

I reported in an uneasy frame of mind. But the very first words of the skipper showed that if he had not forgotten he at least was willing to overlook things. Presently he convinced me that he was really kindly disposed towards me. I was to go to Paris and fly some machines to the squadron. That was good news. I would be able to live in Paris off and on, and right there I made

## LEARNING TO FLY

up my mind that I would square everything and see if I could not hold that job for a long time.

I flew three machines to the school without anything happening, but I was not so lucky with the fourth.

Leaving Paris in the direction of our aerodrome one has to fly over a forest which offers no opportunities at all for landing. It is a thirty-minute trip across that stretch of ground, and I was in the habit of flying high so that in case anything should happen to my machine I would have room enough to glide down into a field outside the woods.

I was over that forest with my fourth machine when of a sudden my engine stopped. I began to glide and looked for an open spot in which I could land. Finally my eyes fell on what I was looking for.

As seen from above, the spot I had selected appeared to be a lawn, but as I came nearer to it I began to see hop poles; however, I was now so low that I had to continue. I landed slap-bang in that hop field and the mess I made of those little poles for a distance of about one hundred feet was great.

But the machine was a mess as well. The poles had gone through the planes and through the body—through everything, in fact. A couple of them had gone through my clothing. I pulled them out and then I climbed out of the car to review the remains of what once had been a perfectly good aeroplane.

Presently the owner of the field came out with a gun. He wanted to know what I was doing in his field. I explained to him that I had had engine trouble, and that he could make out a bill of damages then and there for me to sign. This he did. The man then helped me get the machine into an open field, but before we succeeded in doing that more damage had been done to the hops. It was a day's job and it was dark before we got the bus out.

After that I had to telephone my commanding officer and tell him of the accident, and have a wrecking lorry sent to my assistance. He said he would send some men and a wrecking lorry.

We dismantled the bus, loaded her on the lorry and took her to the aerodrome.

The chances that I would lose my assign-

## LEARNING TO FLY

ment in Paris seemed very good. But the skipper was nice about it. Instead of firing me peremptorily he sent me back.

On the next trip I had an excitable French sergeant, who insisted that I should take him to another flying school. It was only sixty miles out of my way so I consented. But it seemed like waiting for Christmas before we arrived at the aerodrome at about 5:30 in the afternoon. The weather was raw, and I thought I would warm myself while the mechanicians were busy filling the gasoline tanks of my machine. Before I was ready to start it was too dark. I would have to stay over night in that camp, and since I could find no accommodations there I decided to go into a little town nearby. Some of the French flying men were staying there.

I met them. They had never met a khaki flying officer before and insisted upon entertaining me. I was wined and dined and had a splendid time all around. I reached the aerodrome of the squadron without trouble, but found that another man had been sent to Paris to take my place. I was to fly south to another school with a bus. On returning from

## THE FLYING FIGHTER

the southern school I was sent to Paris to fly a French machine back to our school. I met boys at the school who pleased me very much. I received my railway warrant which passed me free on any train going from A—— to Paris, and with my haversack containing my shaving tackle and clean collars and pajamas, I started off. I reached Paris about 9 at night on a pitch black night, which was made worse by a nice, heavy rain; so with the idea that the weather would not be fit for flying the next morning, I started out to see the sights. I took in the Follies and the Alhambra and then went to my hotel.

I did not put in a call to be awakened at any special time, feeling sure it would be raining in the morning. I slept like a log.

At 9:00 in the morning I was rudely torn from my dreams and presented with a wire which came from my Squadron commanding officer stating that I must be home as soon as possible. I looked out of the window and though the rain had stopped, the sky was heavy and the clouds were low. But orders are orders. I decided to fly the machine back as soon as possible.

## LEARNING TO FLY

With this in mind I called up the French aircraft park and told the officer in charge to have the machine ready as I was coming right down to fly it away. I then called up the Paris Naval station to send a car down to take me out to the park. In the interval of waiting I dressed, had breakfast, and when the car rolled up to the hotel door I was ready.

As I got into the car it was just starting to rain, and by the time we got out to the flying grounds it was pouring again. On arriving I put on my flying clothes and asked where my machine was. I was taken to it and on examining it found it to be wet through.

I had made up my mind to fly away that morning at all costs, so as soon as the rain showed signs of letting up, I climbed into the bus, found a couple of mechanics and started to try to get my engine working.

The French way of starting an engine is quite different from ours. Our mechanics would shout:

"Switch off, petrol on, air closed, suck in!" and after a good charge of gasoline vapor had been sucked in by turning the propeller by hand, they would shout:

"Contact!" whereupon the pilot applied the switch.

They would then give the propeller a pull over until they felt a cylinder on compression. Giving the propeller a smart pull now, the cylinder would be forced over compression, and, getting the required spark, the engine would start.

But the French had ways of their own, and it took us about an hour to start the engine, which would only hit on about half its required cylinders. I had to shut down and have it looked over and after another hour we got it started again.

The motor was not all that could be desired in the way of a smooth running engine, but I decided to take a chance on it. I had mapped out the course I was going to take and put my map alongside the seat where it would be handy.

I taxied to the far end of the aerodrome and got into the wind, which was coming right over the top of the hangars, and took off, when, without any warning, my engine

## LEARNING TO FLY

stopped. I was about fifty feet off the ground. Not being a balloon I had to come down and I could not turn as I hadn't enough height. There was nothing to it but land on top of the hangars, and I did.

The roofs were made of canvas and I flew for a center beam which I thought would bear the weight of the machine. I miscalculated, however, and landed between two of them. It was all done so fast that I did not have time to get scared, and before I knew it I was pinned upside down underneath the machine and inside the hangar. The wings of the machine had been left on top and I came on through with the fussalage of the machine, which had turned while coming through the roof and landed on its back with me underneath. The gang of workmen saw the fall and rushed over, rolled the machine over to its natural position and pulled me out. I had had my right shoulder bruised somewhat, but it did not hurt very much.

I reported to the officer in charge, with the log books of the machine. He asked me if I were still set on flying away and on my answering "yes," he gave me the books for another machine. This one was dry. We had no trouble starting the engine and I was mighty glad when I found myself about five thousand feet over the aerodrome.

I was not even then done with my hard luck, for, on getting about forty miles from the 'drome, I ran into a rain storm. In order to dodge it I had to fly about twenty miles in a roundabout way. I eventually got back into my proper course, but I had gone along for only an hour, when I was driven to within a hundred feet of the ground by fog. I could not see two fields ahead of me, but bent upon getting to the squadron as soon as I could, I kept on flying. Soon I had lost my way, so that I had to steer by my compass.

I wanted to reach my destination as quickly as possible, but when my gasoline ran out I had to land, and when I did I found I was fifty miles out of my course. My compass had not been swung to the machine and was useless. I obtained some gasoline and oil and as soon as the fog lifted I got under way again, after being tossed around by the bumps that prevail after rains. I finally came in sight of the naval aerodrome. I was mighty

## LEARNING TO FLY

thankful the trip was over, as my right shoulder, which seemed to be getting worse, was beginning to hurt badly, and I was thankful to climb on board a good old train and start for home.

When I returned from this eventful trip I was sent to England to take a post-graduation course prior to going on active service in France. I reported and was detailed to a squadron in the north of England.

There I met old Beaw, a chap with whom I had been an observer in the first squadron I was with in France. A Yank named Ham from Toronto and a few others made up the greatest squadron I had ever been in. They were always happy and had a commanding officer who was one of the boys and who knew the flying game, having been decorated with the French Legion of Honor and English military crosses. He was an Oxford "blue" and a member of a famous Oxford eight—a gentleman of the highest order.

Within a short time I had flown every war type of machine they had in the place. I perfected myself in dropping bombs and learned how to take photographs.

## THE FLYING FIGHTER

It was at this camp that I took my first solo flight at night. I had been up at night before as a gunner in France, and had some idea what it was like to fly in the dark. Three of us were to go up that night; I was the second.

The route was once around the aerodrome, then land and go up again for another turn around the aerodrome.

The man who was to be No. 1 had no trouble carrying out this program. The flares were up and so arranged as to show the wind direction.

It got to be my turn. In flying at night, and reasonably close to the ground, the aviator can make out woods, roads, lakes and rivers, and the lights in houses. Going up and flying is a simple matter, but coming down in the dark is quite a different thing. The last twenty-five feet of the descent is usually made with nerves on edge. It is impossible in the night to judge distance to the ground and careful judgment is needed to avoid a pile-up.

Night flights in this aerodrome had on previous occasions resulted in the "crow act in the hedge," as we call it, when a man lands

## LEARNING TO FLY

his machine on top of a tree. I wished to avoid that, if possible, and surveyed the surroundings of the aerodrome carefully before I went up.

The first spin around the aerodrome and the first landing were made in very good form. But while going around the second time my engine started to cut out and I came near making a forced landing on the roof of the sheds.

There were a few other stunts I had to do and then I was given my graduation certificate and my wings. That meant that I had to take down my flying "O," which stands for observer.

## CHAPTER XVI

### STUNTS AND ACCIDENTS

I HAD hoped that I would be sent to France immediately, but instead of that I was made an instructor. There were all classes of men in my group. Two of them were particularly interesting. One of them was an Irishman and the other a Scotchman. The men of the squadron looked upon them as "nuts."

The Irishman had been flying slow buses and when put on a fast one threatened to hurt himself. However, the instructor had patience with him, as he was a decent fellow. After about two weeks of dual instruction, he was sent up solo, being warned to be careful and to put on proportionate bank and rudder while making a turn. He was further instructed not to stay up any longer than twenty minutes.

The Irishman started off and flew straightways from the aerodrome towards the coast.

## STUNTS AND ACCIDENTS

The instructor waited and waited and after a while became anxious. The twenty minutes were up and there was no sign of the Irishman. There was nothing to do but to start after him.

But Copper, as the Irishman was known on account of the color of his hair, could not be found. I was wondering what had happened to Copper when an orderly rushed into my room of a sudden and said that somebody wanted to speak on the telephone to the instructor who had gone after Copper. I went to answer the telephone.

"Hello, who's this?" I shouted into the receiver.

"This is the commander of destroyer so and so," came the reply.

"I want to inform you," he went on, "that I picked up a man out at sea, flying machine No. 2464-A. I found him ten miles out. He says he is known in the camp as Copper."

"Is he hurt?" I asked.

"No, he's thawing out down in the engine room and drinking rum. You had better send transportation for him and his machine. Good-bye."

## THE FLYING FIGHTER

Meanwhile Copper's instructor had come down and I told him what had happened. We had to send transportation to Copper, and when the commander of the destroyer was finally relieved of his unexpected company he found he missed Copper's Irish wit very much.

On the following day Copper turned up. His instructor gave him a rather warm reception.

"What in the name of blazes were you trying out at sea, anyway?" he asked.

"Well," said Copper, "once I got up I forgot what you told me, and when I tried to turn the damn thing I landed in the sea."

"What did you go out to sea for?"

"Well," remarked Copper, "I thought that in case I did come down it would be a softer place to land, and the only mistake I made was that I went out too far before trying to turn."

The Scotchman, in trying to have a look at his native land while up in the air, had his first landing in the Scotch hills owing to engine failure. He called us up on the telephone and I was sent out to get his machine.

## STUNTS AND ACCIDENTS

I took a lorry, knowing the funny things these Huns of ours hit, having been one myself, and when I got up to that machine it was just hanging between two trees which kept it from falling over a cliff.

Two hundred feet below that cliff was a waste of rocks, and yet the Scotchman had the nerve to tell the commanding officer that he had made a good landing. It was a good landing, all right. I had to dismantle the bus and carry it to the road and take it home on the lorry.

Oh, we had some merry times in that squadron. One of the instructors used to go out over the town every morning and loop over a monument in the main street. It never occurred to him that this might give the townspeople heart failure; however, he had to have his fun.

Before getting off on this particular morning, the machine of the instructor, while taxiing across the ground, had picked up considerable mud and grass with its tail skid. The mud stayed there all right and while the instructor was making his customary loop it fell off, crashed through the skylight of a

## THE FLYING FIGHTER

large store and caused much consternation. The funny part of it was that the owner of the store thought the flyer had done it on purpose. He made a report to the Government and we received an order not to fly over that town again unless it was absolutely necessary.

Our friend Copper did honor to his name one day by coming in over the sheds too low and putting his tail skid through one of our skylights. In doing that he broke the glass of the skylights and it fell on two buses and cut them up considerably. Not satisfied with that, Copper took away the flagpole, carried off the flag, and smashed his prop doing it. Then he landed, calmly got out of the bus, picked up the flag and flagpole, and walked up to an orderly whom he ordered to put the things back in place.

Scottie was flying along the railroad one day, chasing the Scotch express, which was traveling at the rate of sixty miles an hour. He was trying to put the wind up the back of the engineer by swooping over the engine. That was all right, but the trouble was that Scottie forgot there were telegraph

## STUNTS AND ACCIDENTS

wires on the other side of the track. He slam-banged into them and wrecked this line of communication for three days. As a result of this fine exploit more drastic orders about low flying were issued.

After that we went further away from the 'drome when we wanted to do stunts. Not far from the aerodrome were a number of shooting estates. We would picket men with shotguns on the edge of the 'drome and one of us would fly over the ground and woods to scare up game, which consisted for the greater part of pheasants, partridges and hares. The snipers would do the rest. It was good fun until Robinson, a young pilot, had engine trouble and landed in the middle of a little wood on the estate. We had to cut a road through the trees to get the machine out. It cost the Government real money to get that machine back.

After that the men higher up put their foot down and stopped our little hunt. But being full of spirit the boys had a lot of fun anyway crashing around in the atmosphere. Some of them used to leave camp with the statement that they were going to tea somewhere, and then we would not see them for two days. Ham and I went up quite a number of times to see a friend of ours, who was running a little Government saw-mill in the hills. That boy had the finest and most expert taste for good Scotch ever given any man. At first we visited him occasionally only, then we called upon him once a day, and later we saw him twice a day. The reason for our trips into the hills we kept secret for a long while, until we met our friend in town one night. We were careless enough to introduce him to some of the boys and in the course of the conversation they learned why we were so fond of the Government saw-mill.

Before long it was difficult to find an airplane in the aerodrome. In fact, we were seriously considering transferring the establishment to the saw-mill. Then the commanding officer was permitted to share our secret and another diversion of ours had to be abandoned.

One by one the little stunts that used to make life on the training aerodrome so very interesting were lopped off. A general order came forbidding any pilot to do stunts at ele-

## STUNTS AND ACCIDENTS

vations less than 2,000 feet. But we made up for that in other ways.

It was on a Sunday afternoon when I was called to the orderly room of the commanding officer's office. I was told that I was to leave next morning by the 11:30 train for Glasgow, Scotland, whence I would proceed to a little town just outside and receive a machine of the type known as BE2E. I was to fly that machine to a point in the South of England and was to take with me on my trip a chap named Atwood, known in the aerodrome by everybody as "At."

We caught the train, changed at Edinburgh, and found that we had some time to spare before we could get the train for Glasgow. The two of us decided that we would have a look at the town and we did so. We found the place quite interesting and were walking down Princess street when of a sudden we heard a roar, and, looking up, we beheld an aeroplane known as a Rumpty type, flying at about fifty feet above the ground. It was flying over the street, but I don't know yet what the couple of British Huns in it were trying to do. The machine in question is large and slow and flies steadily enough. At one end of the street there is a square and in that square stands a monument. The Rumpty "zoomed" over it and missed its top by a few inches. Then it went on. We learned afterwards that the machine had landed somewhere further down the street. Cold shivers ran down my back while I was looking at the foolhardy stunts of the men in the machine, but the people looking on were impressed only by the daring of these bold British birdmen.

Arriving at Glasgow that night we called up the aerodrome and let the commanding officer know that we had arrived. Next morning an automobile called for us and we were taken to the aerodrome, which lies near the factory where these machines are made.

"At" and I got into the machine we were to take south, though neither of us liked the looks of the weather. A storm was coming up, but rather than lose time we decided to go over the tops of the clouds.

Before we had gotten beyond the clouds we were up 10,000 feet and it certainly was cold up there. After that we headed for the hills in the south and we had to go up a little more

## STUNTS AND ACCIDENTS

in order to have enough gliding room in case something should happen to the machine. I have always found it the best policy to fly as high as possible when using a machine whose knacks and tricks I am not familiar with. The prospect of landing in those snow-covered hills did not appeal to us.

I froze a toe and part of my nose, but aside from that nothing happened. The machine was safely delivered at our aerodrome. We had lunch and got thawed out, and then started up again to take the buses on to their destination. We had gone quite a way south when more trouble came. We ran into a fog. Ground fogs are the worst enemy of the aviator. In addition to blotting out the marks by which he steers, they also make it impossible for him to find suitable landing places in case of necessity. No pilot likes to fly in a fog, but when he has to he generally holds close enough to the ground to enable him to see at least a little.

In a long distance flight we generally go over the top of the fog and then find our bearings by means of the compass and the timing of the speed we are making.

## THE FLYING FIGHTER

But we were not so very far away from the point at which we were to land the machines to be refilled with gas and oil, and for that reason going to the top of the fog was out of the question. I hugged the ground as closely as possible and in so doing made as a first discovery that there are large manufacturing towns somewhere in the middle of England. I was going along at low speed when suddenly there loomed up before me, out of the fog, something that caused my heart to stop beating. Right in front of me stood a large and tall factory chimney.

I turned to the right to avoid it, but I had hardly done that when I was close to another chimney, which was directly in my path. Once more I turned. But before I had gone very far I was up against another chimney. I turned again; another chimney. I decided to see if I could not get out of the forest of chimneys by going in the other direction, but that too had the same result—more chimneys. For the next and longest ten minutes I ever experienced I described circles and half-circles around chimneys with the machine now

## STUNTS AND ACCIDENTS

on her nose, then on her tail, when not on her side. I finally reached what I thought an open place and then decided to go over the top of the chimneys.

One of my reasons for staying so close to the ground was that I wanted to keep in sight of the railroad track which had served as my guide. The weather was so thick that I could not see two fields ahead of me.

When I came close to the ground again after sailing over the chimneys I found that I had lost the railroads, as well as At and his bus; for I afterwards found out that he had landed some 20 miles behind to avoid risks.

There was no use in going on, because, for all I knew I might run into more chimneys and not get off so luckily the next time. With that in mind I decided to land in the first open field I came to. I came to one before long and landed. Soon hundreds of people had gathered around the machine and amused themselves by writing their names on its planes with lead pencil. One yokel was enterprising enough to cut a piece out of a strut with his knife. I had a hard time fighting these souvenir hunters, and I am sure that they would have carted off the machine bodily had it not been for an officer of the law, known in England as Bobby, who came and helped me stave off the memento-hungry mob.

The officers told me that there was an aerodrome five miles down the road. From the minute directions he gave me I gathered that I would be able to make those five miles despite the fog.

I had some trouble getting that mob out of the way, but succeeded in the end. I started the motor, asked some of the men to hold the machine back until I should signal them to release it, and then climbed in. I taxied to the other side of the field to get into the wind. The crowd closed in behind me and when I turned around to take off, the onlookers scampered to the sides of the field. I opened up the throttle and was just getting off the ground when a little girl rushed out in front of the machine, which was then going about sixty miles an hour.

The only way to save the girl's life was to take a chance on my own neck. Before I knew it I had hurtled over the little girl, missing her by a few inches with the under

## STUNTS AND ACCIDENTS

carriage of the machine. I was going at such a speed that had she been hit by any part of the machine at all she would have been killed. In getting over the little girl I lost my flying speed and a bus without flying speed is like so much lead. The result was that I crashed into a hedge, smashed my prop to bits, and then the machine landed on its nose in the next field. The motor was making about 2,200 revolutions a minute, and to make things worse the gasoline tanks piled upon it and were ignited. Within a second the entire machine was ablaze. I was caught in some debris of the machine about ten feet away from the part that was burning. But I had sense enough to save my haversack, in which I carried my shaving tackle and my pajamas. I also thought of my stick. Next I seized the pyrene syringe and hurried over to the fire, which I succeeded in putting out. By that time a number of Home Defense Guards had appeared on the scene, though the only thing they found to do was to keep the people out of the field.

I had made a fine mess of it.

After that I made a trip to the nearest

telephone three miles away and called up the wrecking crew of the aerodrome. They were to come up and salve the remains of a perfectly good BE2E.

This was my first real crash as a full-fledged pilot.

After that I went to a hotel, had a bath, and examined myself for broken parts. But aside from a good shaking up I had suffered no injury. My companion, the haversack, also was in good shape.

Next morning the commanding officer of the aerodrome sent over the wrecking lorry and a crew of students to pick up the odds and ends. Some of the students were Canadians and when later we met again at the 'drome they entertained me royally.

I could not leave that aerodrome until word had come from the commander of my squadron that I was to be relieved and sent back. But I had to wait a couple of days for my orders, being meanwhile billeted in a hotel in the city. I put in my free time hanging around the aerodrome and watching the boys tearing through the air learning to fly. While doing that I had occasion to find out

## STUNTS AND ACCIDENTS

that I was not the only one who had done queer things on his first solo trips.

One of the boys at this aerodrome—I have forgotten his name—was coming over a building about 70 feet high. On one corner of the building there was a small tower on whose top had been placed a weather vane resembling a rooster. The apprentice pilot was sailing a little too low, caught the rooster with one of his planes, and went down in the court behind a house a short way off, complete with rooster.

The machine was completely demolished and we thought that the man had surely been killed. The aerodrome ambulance rushed off to the scene of the accident as fast as it could, but the man was found calmly sitting on the wreck of his machine smoking the inevitable cigarette. There was a smile on his face as he pointed to the rooster.

"I always did want to see that thing at close range," he said, "but I did not want to bring it home with me."

I knew several of the boys at this school and found that they were learning to fly R. E. 8's, a machine that has the reputation of being very tricky. Its main fault is that it is hard to keep from spinning, much to the discomfort of the budding pilot.

I noticed that though the weather was bad and cloudy, it being a raw spring day, there was no let-up in the work of this aerodrome. Pilots were then in great demand in France and training had to go on in almost any kind of weather.

Venabels, one of the chaps I knew, had just been transferred from the squadron I was attached to. He was now flying an R. E. 8 and seemed quite proud of his accomplishment. He was going to fly one of these machines to-day, he said, for the special benefit of the wing commander, and started to do so.

He left the ground in pretty good shape and then went straight up. At about 300 feet he tried to turn and then the machine went for a spinning nose dive. Before its pilot could right it again it had hit the ground and immediately burst into flame. Before we could get to the man he had been burned to death. Accidents will happen, of course, but it made me sick to think about it, for he was

## STUNTS AND ACCIDENTS

one of my best friends. And I always hate to see them go that way.

Next morning I got into touch with my commanding officer and he gave me orders to go to another factory for another machine. This time I had a bus of greater power and made a successful trip. After signing the machine over to the receiving squadron I reported to my own squadron and was sent back to the same factory to deliver another machine. This time I had a mechanic with me. In the afternoon we landed at a squadron to fill our tanks and get some food. After that we resumed our journey. We had flown about an hour and a half when we were overtaken by a rain-storm. It was getting late and for that reason I decided to land and come down at Melton Mowbray, the world-famed home of English pork pies and fox hunting. We put the machine away for the night and went to a large farmhouse where we were received with open arms and well entertained. The weather being bad, the next day we went fox hunting. I put in a pleasant day on a postage-stamp saddle, and all that night I was sore and slept hardly at all.

## THE FLYING FIGHTER

It was very windy next day but despite that I decided to finish the trip. The clouds were low.

As we started off I broke a king post on an aileron, just as I was getting off the ground. I spliced and splinted it and made a successful second start, reaching my destination about 3:00 in the afternoon, after a very strenuous trip.

## CHAPTER XVII

### AIR BATTLES OVER THE LINES

Upon reporting to the park commander, I found that seven of us, myself included, had been detailed for overseas duty, which meant France, and that we were to take seven machines with us.

I returned to the squadron and on the following day the seven of us started. We took with us our mascot, a fox terrier puppy about six weeks old. Pup was wrapped up in mufflers and fur helmet and, thus equipped, was a passenger in the wireless box in Ham's bus.

Though the weather was bad, we started out, but we had not gone very far before we realized that we would have to fly over the tops of the clouds at an altitude of about 12,000 feet.

It was a splendid sight to see the seven machines, six with two men and one with two

## THE FLYING FIGHTER

men and a dog, dodging around the big white peaks of the upper world.

As we sped along we came to a hole in the clouds and peeping down I spied an aerodrome I knew very well. It occurred to me that the gang would like to be taken down there to feed the pup and fill up with juice and oil.

I went down in a nose dive and the others followed suit.

We landed, one after the other, took our supplies and stretched our cramped limbs, and, after feeding the dog with milk, started up again. The hole in the clouds had not closed up meanwhile so we went through it once more.

We had gone about an hour or so when I noticed that my pressure valve was acting queerly. Next the engine stopped.

I began to use the hand pump to keep the motor running until I could get to a place where I could see the ground. But that seemed quite impossible. The speed of the engine was now so low that I was falling anyway, so I stopped and dived downward through thick clouds in a glorious plunge at

## AIR BATTLES OVER THE LINES

about 140 miles an hour. Then I righted the machine, picked out a field to land in, and began to pump again like mad in order to keep my engine running until I landed. It had been my intention to fix my motor and then join the others. I was hard at work when suddenly I heard above me the whirr of propellers, and, looking up, saw that the other six were coming down also. The field was none too large and I swallowed my heart several times, as they came in to land, but they all got down safely.

While my mechanician was busy on the valves, I consulted my maps to find where we were. I discovered that we were about ten miles from an aerodrome and told the boys that they had better start for it. There was a tall row of trees on the windward side of the field, which we had to "zoom" on getting off the field, and once more I swallowed my heart, as they started off, but no accidents happened. By the time the last one was on his wings my engine was running again and I started after them.

At the aerodrome we had something to eat and then we started off again, though it had begun to snow. The falling snow prevented our seeing very far and before long only three of us were together, the other four having disappeared. As we neared F—— one of the boys had water trouble and, on landing, he hit a tree and landed on the ground in a crash, nearly killing himself and his mechanician. The others arrived safely.

Upon reporting at the "War House" in London, as we called our general headquarters, we were given two days' leave and then told to return north as ferry pilots. The work of the ferry pilot consists of delivering machines from one part of the country to another, such as we had been doing for a short time.

That was a rude shock to us. We had bid our friends in the north good-bye under the impression that we would immediately go to France, and now we were to spend more time trundling machines from one part of the country to another. Well, we did our best to drown our sorrows during these two days' leave. Finally, our commanding officer gave us a little dinner to help us get over our disappointment. To make sure that none of

## AIR BATTLES OVER THE LINES

us would grieve any longer from not being able to go to France he also took us to a show. The same night, flat broke, having enjoyed ourselves, we caught a train for the north and arrived at our aerodrome in the morning, much to the surprise of our friends.

Four days later we received orders to again report at the "War House," which is located in the "Big Smoke." On arriving there I met an old Yankee friend of mine and he greeted me with the remark:

"How do you like the 'Big Smoke,' anyway?"

Ever since then I have associated this name with London.

That man's name, by the way, was Libby. He is a Texan, and, like myself, is fond of adventure. I had been able once to do Libby a favor. Libby had made up his mind to fight for the French, or at least drive a motor truck for them, but the mechanical examiners were not going to take him. I went to the commanding officer and told him that Libby, though he might not know much about a motor now, was sure to learn quickly, and

## THE FLYING FIGHTER

that I would see to it that he made himself a useful man.

The commanding officer thought it over for a long time and finally let me have "Lib." He proved that he was a clever chap and before long was one of the best drivers. When we went to France Libby was one of the company. We had not been over there long when he fell ill with pneumonia. The weather there did not seem to agree with us and "Lib" was sent back to England.

When he recovered he was sent back to France with a repair unit, and, when next I met him, he told me he was trying for the Flying Corps. I had just managed to get my own papers for the same corps and told Libby how to go about it. He had action on his petition very soon and became an officer on probation in the Flying Corps shortly after I did. He was sent to a squadron, and during his period of observation he and his pilot shot down ten Huns, for which they each received the military cross. He was later sent back to England to become a pilot, went back to France and shot down ten other Huns. Libby was some fighter, as the saying goes, and he was soon made a captain; I felt proud to have him for a pal.

At the "War House" I was informed that I had been assigned to a scout and fighting squadron doing service in France. I would now have another opportunity to fight the Huns.

Arriving in France I was given a machine of the Spad type. I began to fly the machine to discover its moods and tricks, and then had it adjusted to suit my way of flying. My first turn of service at the front as a pilot consisted of patrol work for three days running. It was an uneventful start. On the fourth day I went up again on patrol to 20,000 feet. I was looking for Huns up there, but found none. Since it was very cold I decided to go down a way, and shut off my power.

At the level of 18,000 feet, I found myself sweeping along a very large peak of cloud. Intending to spoil its pretty formation I dived into it, and, coming out on the other side, found myself alongside of a Hun plane of the Albatross type. I had no intimation at all that a Hun was present and I guess he

## THE FLYING FIGHTER

was in the same position. I suppose he was as much surprised as I was when he saw me emerging from the cloud. That he was surprised was indicated by his failure to open fire upon me after coming alongside of him. Neither of us could shoot at the other for the reason that the guns of the machines we were flying were fixed to the machine so that the machine itself has to be pointed.

We were so close together that this could not be done without our ramming one another, which both of us had to avoid if we did not wish to crash to the earth together.

The Hun waved at me and I waved at him.

We found ourselves in a very peculiar situation. I was so close to him that I could see with the naked eye every detail of his machine. His face also I could see quite clearly, even to the wrinkles around his mouth.

There was something odd in our position. I had to smile at the thought that we were so close together and yet dared not harm one another. The Hun also smiled. Then I reached down to feel the handle on my pressure reservoir to make sure that it was in its

## AIR BATTLES OVER THE LINES

proper place, for I knew that one of us would soon have to make a break.

I had never before met a Hun at such close quarters in the air and though we flew parallel to one another for only a few minutes, the time seemed like a week. I remembered some of the tactics told me by some of the older and best fighters in the corps, and was wondering how I could employ them. Finally a thought occurred to me. Two machines flying at the same height are not necessarily on exactly the same level, as they keep going up and down for about 20 feet.

I was flying between the Hun and his own lines and I had fuel for another hour and a quarter anyway. I wanted to make sure of this bird, but decided to play a waiting game. We continued our flight side by side.

After a while, however, much sooner than I expected, the Hun began to get restless and started to manœuvre for position; like myself he was utilizing the veriest fraction of every little opportunity in his endeavor to out-manœuvre the antagonist. Finally, the Hun thought he had gotten the lead.

I noticed that he was trying to side-slip,

## THE FLYING FIGHTER

go down a little, evidently for the purpose of shooting me from underneath, but not far enough for me to get a dive on him. I was not quite sure as yet that such was really his intention, but the man was quick. Before I knew what had happened he had managed to put five shots into my machine, but all of them missed me.

I manœuvred into an offensive position as quickly as I could, and before the Hun could fire again I had my machine gun pelting him. My judgment must have been fairly good.

The Hun began to spin earthward. I followed to finish him, keeping in mind, meanwhile, that it is an old game in flying to let the other man think you are hit. This bit of strategy will often give an opportunity to get into a position that will give you the drop on your antagonist. The ruse is also sometimes used to get out of a fight when in trouble with gun jam, or when bothered by a defective motor.

I discovered soon that this precaution was not necessary, for the Hun kept spinning down to the ground. He landed with a crash.

A few minutes later I landed two fields

## AIR BATTLES OVER THE LINES

away from the wreck and ran over to see the kill I had made.

I had hit the Hun about fifty times and had nearly cut off both his legs at the hips.

There was nothing left in the line of souvenirs, as the Tommies had gotten to the wreck before I did. I carried off a piece of his props and had a stick made of it. That night we had a celebration over the first Hun I had brought down behind our own line since I became a pilot.

Next day I went out to get another Hun to add to my collection. I was in the act of crossing the Hun lines when, bang! to the right of me came a thud, and my engine stopped. Revenge, I thought. I volplaned to the ground, made a good landing in a field just behind our lines, and, 'phoning up the squad, I then had another engine brought out to replace mine.

On my way to the squadron I witnessed one of the greatest air fights I have ever seen. It took place above the cemetery of P——.

Three Huns were aloft behind their own lines, and back of them was one of our patroling scouts.

## THE FLYING FIGHTER

The Hun does not believe in coming over our lines if he can possibly help it, and generally he will manœuvre so that any engagement will have to be waged over German territory.

One of our men named Price, who was coming in from patrol, was pilot of the scout, which was flying at the same height as the Hun aircraft, about 12,000 feet. Price was well behind the Hun lines when they saw him, and all three of them made for him at once. I happened to be at an artillery observation post, which I had to pass on my way home, and so was able to get a good view of the combat.

The foremost of the Huns made straight for Price, and for a minute it looked as though he intended ramming him. The combatants separated again and began to fire upon one another, as the tut-tut-tut of the machine guns told me. Of a sudden one Hun volplaned, while another made straight for Price. I wondered what Price would do, but saw the next moment that he had "zoomed" over the second Hun machine, which just then swooped down upon him. While Price was "zooming," I noticed that the first Hun was falling to the ground, having either been disabled or killed by Price's machine gun.

Yet within a few moments the second Hun also crashed to earth, and the third was now making for home as fast as his motor would carry him; but Price chased and quickly caught up with him. It was an exciting race. Price was working his machine gun for all the thing was worth, and before long the third Hun went down.

Just five minutes had been required for the fight. When I met Price later I congratulated him. I remember wishing him all the good luck a fellow could have. But that did not help, for within a month he, too, came down in a heap.

The day following the fight I went out on another patrol, and, remembering what had happened on the day before, I decided to go up high before sailing over into Hunland. The Huns were in the habit of being especially hard on our fellows after such an exploit as Price's, and I knew that I would have to keep all of my wits about me that day.

## THE FLYING FIGHTER

I went up to about 15,000 feet and started across the lines.

I had no trouble getting across Hunland. But the day was fairly clear and the Hun "Archies," I soon discovered, were working overtime. The amount of shrapnel ammunition they spent that day was not small. I was about three miles behind the Hun lines, when right ahead of me exploded a "woolly bear." It was all black smoke, with a heart of fire and ragged at the edges. When it burst my machine started to do a cake-walk. It seemed to be out of control. The racing motor caused such vibrations that I was afraid the machine would fall to pieces. I shut off power quickly and headed homeward, landing in one of our advance landing grounds.

The trouble was that one half of a propeller blade had been shot away. Otherwise the machine was unhurt. I telephoned for another propeller and was soon up in the air again.

I will admit that I had the greatest respect for the Hun "Archie" batteries. The "woolly bear" they had fired at me was

## AIR BATTLES OVER THE LINES

something new, and it certainly did damage enough when it exploded near a machine.

But duty is duty.

After the mechanics had attached the propeller I went up again, but shrunk at least six inches when the next "woolly bear" exploded quite close to me. I ducked into the cockpit, although it is self-evident that one is no safer in the cockpit than outside. When the machine crashes to the ground the cockpit goes along, since no one as yet has devised any means of anchoring it to a cloud. Though the bus I was flying was a fast one, that Hun "Archie" battery did most creditable work. I must say that much for the Hun, though I hate him like poison.

The Huns were good shots, even at the elevation at which I was flying, where my machine as seen from the ground appeared no larger than a mosquito. I spent a very exciting day. The fire of the Hun "Archies" had never been as accurate as to-day and those "woolly bears" seemed to have us all puzzled.

For all that, I had been lucky. When I returned to the aerodrome it was to learn that "Pizzdoodle," an old Scotch friend of mine and as fine a boy as ever lived, had been brought down.

Capt. Albert Ball, one of the best pilots in the corps and with more Huns to his credit than any one else, had also been killed. The same fate had overtaken a number of others, many of whom I knew.

I spent a great deal of time that night wondering whether it would be my turn next. I remember looking over my medals and a certain peculiar mascot of mine—a Chinese doll. Life never seemed so uncertain nor so short.

I had to wait next morning for quite some time before I received orders to go on patrol. In the meantime I had learned that the King was coming to inspect our squadron, and I wondered whether I would have to hie myself into the blue just at that time and so be obliged to miss the show. But luck was with me this time and I stayed below.

Presently the King drove up in a car. We were lined up and were looked over by the royal eye. The King shook hands with the commanding officer, chatted with him for a while, and then walked down our line. We were presented to him one by one, and the King had a kind word and a smile for every man.

After the King had addressed the man next to me, the wing commander told him that I was a Yankee; whereupon the King shook hands heartily with me and told me that he was proud of the Americans in the British service.

He asked me how I liked flying, and I told him that I had had no fair chance as yet, having been shot down only twice. The King laughed heartily and remarked that he had no fear for me, that I seemed quite able to take care of myself. He also gave it as his opinion that the United States of America would soon be doing fine work and giving a good account of itself. Then he questioned me as to my length in the service, and expressed the hope that we might meet again.

When the King had left our camp, I started out on patrol with a feeling that something was bound to happen that day. I was rather blue, but I made up my mind that old "Archie," back of the Hun lines, was not going to get me this time if I could possibly help it.

I went up to 20,000 feet, and soon noticed that there was a fight under way across the Hun lines. I wanted to see what was going on and made for the spot, but I had not gone very far before old "woolly bear" picked us up. Soon the shells were bursting all around me.

Before long a gang of our men were making for the scene of the fight and this gave the Hun "Archies" every reason for sending up their "woolly bears."

The seventh shell that exploded near me sent a steel fragment into my carbureter. Of a sudden my motor slowed down, and, as usual, I had visions of having to make a forced landing in Hunland.

The piece of the shell had done considerable damage to the sides of the cockpit, and for a moment I feared that it had smashed some of my control. But that fear was ungrounded, as presently I discovered. My controls were still intact, and for that reason I would be able to glide to the ground. I swung my machine into position for a glide

## AIR BATTLES OVER THE LINES

towards our line, and before very long I was at 10,000 feet, with the Hun shells keeping close to my track. Some of them exploded a little ahead of me, which is always a bad sign for a descending man. It shows that the "Archie" gunners have a good line on the course of the dive, and every next shell may be the last for the man in the machine.

It was bad going on this day. The "woolly bears" continued to stand in my way, and I sped through their fumes nearly all the way down. To this day I do not understand how I managed to land, as I finally did, in a convenient field.

But forced landings keep a man's nerves on edge. With the motor dead the pilot has lost the full power to control the machine when judging his landing place, and generally he reaches the ground at too great a speed to make a safe landing.

On this occasion I hit the ground at a speed of about 55 miles per hour, and had the misfortune of being thrown to one side by a bump on the ground which was struck by one of the wheels. The next instant the machine was on its nose, and then turned over on its back, and more or less smashed. During the somersault I was stunned by being thrown against the instrument board. The result was that I was bruised all over, and had my lip cut, my eyes blackened, and my chin knocked up quite badly. I was unable to get out of the wreckage, and still had to fear that the gasoline, which was spilling from the tanks, would ignite; in which case I would have met the end which a pilot fears most.

After I had been pulled from the wreck, I was given some badly needed attention by a doctor who was passing; then I went to the nearest telephone and called up the commanding officer, who had me brought to the aerodrome in a car. He also sent a lorry for the remains of my bus.

That night we had our wing commander for a guest at dinner, and he told me that they were going to send me back to England for a furlough. I wanted to stay, but he thought that it was better that I should rest up a bit, saying if I did not get out now the Huns would soon get me for good. Though I had raised some objection to being returned to England, I was really quite willing to go. I

## AIR BATTLES OVER THE LINES

have yet to meet the flyer who wants to go back in the air after he has had the necessary number of spills, unless he is out of his mind or has imbibed too freely.

The cumulative effect of accidents in flying is such that in the end the man has to fight his nerves as much as the dangers of the air and the Hun. I have known old pilots who had been on active duty at the front for months and months, and nothing seemed to matter to them any more. For all that, they were gradually falling to pieces. They were keeping up physically well enough, but their nerves were getting away from them, and the moment was bound to come when they would not be able to control them any more.

That state of affairs is easily understood when one stops to consider that nine times out of ten the man going over the Hun lines is shelled. On almost every trip he may have to fight some "Heinie," as we call the German aviator. This means that the man aloft is taking chances every minute. The thing that keeps the man buoyed up is the thought that he has become indispensable to the men fighting on the ground. Without the

## THE FLYING FIGHTER

airplane, modern military control would be impossible. The men in the front trenches rely entirely upon the observer and his pilot for their communication during a fight. The flyers know that, of course, and for that reason strain every nerve to be of service to the boys in the trenches. How valuable the services of the flyer are is shown by the fact that often they succeed in cutting down by fifty per cent. the artillery fire of the opponent through "spotting" the friendly artillery to the batteries that are doing the harm

I got my route orders next morning and then started for England. Some of the boys envied me that I could go back to old Blighty, and swore that the next time they went out they would take a chance on being brought down by the Hun "Archies," who used the "woolly bear" shells.

I am inclined to believe that some of them were as good as their word. Within a short time three of them had been brought down for good, and two others had to land on German territory, where they were made prisoners of war.

# CHAPTER XVIII

### BACK TO BLIGHTY

Upon my arrival in England I received a week's leave of absence and when it was over I was detailed to a good squadron near the "Big Smoke."

My new duties consisted of having to test and ferry to other squadrons and training camps all sorts of buses. That took me all over England and in some cases to France.

I enjoyed that work for a while, but soon discovered that it was very strenuous. I was almost constantly in the air, and the bad season was now on. For a while I was laid up with bronchial pneumonia, an ailment which has frequently bothered me.

I made an attempt to be transferred to a better climate as instructor, but there were no openings just then.

Three weeks after my discharge from the hospital I went to work with a new squad.

## THE FLYING FIGHTER

My present detail had another feature which was not welcome to me. I was expected to fly every type of machine which was then being manufactured, and these types were not few in number. The first day in camp one of the pilots, a chap by name of McGurrie, had engine trouble while in a scouting machine, and injured himself in landing. Since just then I was flying the same type of machine I made sure that my motor was O. K. before leaving the ground. But despite that I had the same sort of accident. A few days later one of the fellows got his machine on its back while up in the air, and had a hard time righting it again. He came near landing on his back, which, of course, would have been the end of him.

It was the duty of the men in the squadron camps near London to participate in the manœuvres against the Zeppelin raids. Nine-tenths of the alarms were false; but it was impossible to tell the scares from the real thing, and for that reason we would go up and patrol around until the "all clear" signal came out. Usually that led to very long flights, which was a hardship in many cases,

## BACK TO BLIGHTY

for the reason that we used to go up in whatever clothing we happened to have on when the alarm came in, no time being taken by us to dress. When the alarm signal came, we had to rush for our machines, jump into them, and then get off without delay of any sort. Some of the alarms came at night, of course, and I have seen men climb into their machines in their pajamas. And pajamas are not quite the thing for a three hours' patrol in the air. It is always cold up there, no matter what the season may be, and the speed of the machine intensifies that cold many times. Many of the men almost froze to death, and often they would land because of that before the "all clear" signal came.

I went up once to an elevation of 14,500 feet. I was up there an hour and a half, and, being above the clouds, had no idea where I was. Of a sudden my revolution counter broke and the air pressure in the gasoline tanks gave out. I shut off the engine and started towards the ground. The machine I was in had a flying speed of about seventy miles per hour. That meant that I would have to keep up good speed all the way down.

## THE FLYING FIGHTER

The first stratum of cloud I went through was so wet that a lot of it froze to the machine. It was enormously thick, and for all I knew it might hang only a few hundred feet above the ground. There was the chance that I would emerge from it and find myself over the very center of London, which is as poor a landing field as anybody would care to have. As I was going down, the thought of finding a convenient landing spot plagued my mind constantly.

I had plunged down 5,000 feet, so far as my instrument showed me, and was still in that cloud. I had given up all hope of ever getting out of it when suddenly I dived into clear air and saw the ground. The machine I was flying had a small gliding angle, and I would have to find a landing spot quickly. Having ascertained now that I was not going to drop in the city of London, I was much relieved, but I had some trouble, nevertheless, in discovering a reasonably level space. The machine was plunging towards earth at a terrific speed and I had little time to pick a convenient spot. Nothing upon which my eyes lit seemed to serve the purpose. But finally I found an open space and decided to settle down upon it. I was sure that a good landing could be made, but such was not the case. In striking the ground the machine turned turtle and was rather badly damaged.

While the machine was turning over, I had presence of mind enough to throw myself out of the cockpit. I landed on my head but suffered no injury. To my mind came then a remark made to me by the doctor of the hospital to which I was taken after I had been shot in the head in France.

"It is a lucky thing," said the doctor, "that your head is of solid ivory, and seventeen inches thick; otherwise you would have been killed."

There is no doubt that had it not been for the cast iron constitution which I enjoyed prior to enlisting I would have died long ago.

Old Ham also was working on this aerodrome. One day he took up a big bus for a test and while he was up the engine gave out. He came down suddenly and landed on a railroad track. At the aerodrome a gang of

## THE FLYING FIGHTER

German prisoners were employed to level off the ground surface. They would laugh and jeer every time there was a crash. They did so on this occasion; in fact, they never lost a chance to let us know that their enmity towards us was real enough.

On the day Ham crashed I flew down the coast with a bus to be delivered in France. I made a fine trip, but on getting over the station at which I was to land I shut off power and started to spiral down. Unfortunately, the wind drifted me off, and when I came out of my spiral, at the height of about 500 feet, my engine would not start again.

I tried everything possible to get that motor spinning, but it was no use. I did not have height enough to get over the road, on the other side of which the aerodrome was located. On this side of the road stood some small pine trees and I settled down upon them. Luckily, the trees were small, and their tops formed a gentle cushion for me to land on. The propeller of the machine was slightly damaged, but that was all.

I climbed out of the machine with my bag, stick and log books, and reported at the head-

## BACK TO BLIGHTY

quarters of the aerodrome. The commanding officer happened to be in.

"I have brought you down a DH5, sir," I said.

"Is it any good?" he inquired.

"It's perfectly all right except the engine," I answered.

"Where is it?" asked the officer.

"It's over on the pine trees," I replied. "I cut out the engine when I was away up and then it refused to start again, so I landed the machine in the trees."

For a moment the officer did not know what to say, then he smiled and asked me if I were hurt and offered me a cigarette. After that he signed my log book and gave me a receipt for the machine. I had lunch with him and then returned to my squadron.

Ten days later I had another weird trip. I was up in the air a good many thousand feet and the fog and haze were so thick that I could see very little. Above me there was another layer of cloud, so I decided to get to the top of that and then fly by compass and speed.

Before I reached the top of that cloud

stratum I had ascended to 13,000 feet. Then I headed for my destination, which I knew was about forty minutes distant, if I kept up ordinary speed. I allowed for the time I had taken by going up so high, and after forty minutes' flight on the level I started to descend. I had dived a good ways but could see no ground. The thing began to worry me. I looked at my instrument, and that showed me that I had gone 12,000 feet. Since I had gone up to 13,000 feet I could be no more than 1,000 feet above the earth. But no ground could be seen, and yet when I had gone up the weather had not been thick enough to make it impossible for a man to see that far.

But the weather in England is a most unreliable and treacherous thing. I got down to 300 feet and then the first thing upon which my eyes hit was a building which in another instant I recognized as the town hall of A——. I pulled on the throttle, but the engine did not respond. At that height there is no time for manœuvring, and in this case there was also no room. So I made up my mind to trust to God and then let the bus have her way. I was just about to land in a

## BACK TO BLIGHTY

street, as things looked, when the motor suddenly kicked four or five times and started off. I literally swallowed my heart and sat back in the seat, glad to get that thing out in the open country. I noticed that in some places the clouds were hanging as low as fifty feet above the ground; a young gale was coming from off the sea. But my troubles were not over yet.

There is a regulation which restrains pilots from flying over certain prohibited areas, such as sites occupied by munition plants and works which manufacture high explosives. There are so many of these prohibited areas that it is impossible to remember them all. The man who does not remember them is likely to get shot at by the English "Archies," or reprimanded if caught, and I had to find an aerodrome as soon as possible to avoid these, which I did, and I was very thankful after I was once more on Mother Earth. The same fate may befall the flyer while going over to France. We were required to leave our own coast at an elevation of 5,000 feet and the French had a similar regulation.

## THE FLYING FIGHTER

On one of my first trips to France, made in company with eleven others, we were heading for the Channel at an elevation of nine thousand feet. That caused the English "Archies" to shell us. They were under the impression that we were Huns. But we made ourselves known by coming down to the prescribed level.

As a rule, we returned to England from our trips to France by the Channel boats. But often old machines had to be flown back from the parks in France, and in that case we made our return journey in the air.

We used to do our best to make sure that the machines were in proper shape before starting on a trip. It is not pleasant to land in the middle of the English Channel and float around for an hour or more before a patrol boat picks you up. But it is quite a common occurrence to make forced landings in that body of water. The number of machines turned out in England increased rapidly, and many men were engaged in ferrying them across to France. Though proportionately accidents were few, once in a while the ferry flyers and their machines would never be heard from again.

We had to fly when ordered, and there were times when it made no difference at all what sort of weather prevailed. That depended somewhat on the demand for machines at the front. As the aviation training schools in England multiplied, our work increased by leaps and bounds.

There was also much testing to do. There were days on which the testing pilots, of whom I was one, had to be up continually, and to our commander it made no difference what the state of the weather was. It might rain pitchforks and hammer handles and still our work had to go on. We used to take turns at testing and ferrying, and very often faults of the machine that had not developed during the test would show themselves while we were taking it to its destination. Our measure of experience was getting fuller every day, and some of the things that happened to us were queer indeed; yet it was all in the day's work.

While I was on ferry work between England and France I had a very good chance

## THE FLYING FIGHTER

to observe what the naval flyers had to deal with. In the first place I could see the bottom of the channel the biggest part of the way across. From an altitude of several thousand feet the bed showed up in brownish grey, except for the large deep holes, which appeared blue. It seemed queer that one should be able to see the bottom where big steamships were traveling, and I could easily understand now how the naval airmen could see a submarine when submerged.

This particular search is quite interesting. The patrols, keeping a lookout for hostile craft of that kind, would cruise about until they had spotted one of the "tin fishes." Then they would go down and drop aerial torpedoes on it. If they saw other hostile ships, they would call up the naval station and notify it. A destroyer would be ordered to the scene, and then the naval airmen would help with the bombing. At other times they would watch for hostile aerial coast patrols and raiders bound for various points in France and England. The naval men have become so efficient that it is very seldom that enemy craft of any kind, either on water or in the

## BACK TO BLIGHTY

air, go on reconnaissance without being fought by them. In many instances they have been able to inflict heavy losses upon the Huns.

Besides meeting the difficulties of flying over water, the naval men have to train themselves to land on water, which is quite a ticklish thing to do, for the reason that for the last few feet there is nothing to show what the distance between the machine and the water's surface is, and many a spill occurs in learning. Water is as hard as land to fall on, and not soft, as many seem to think. It will smash a plane as quickly as if it had landed on the ground.

Men who fly on the ground cannot necessarily fly over water. Some men seem to lose their sense of equilibrium when out of sight of land, and, as the sea is such a tremendous body, that is not to be wondered at. Conditions vary a great deal over water and when correcting bumps or small erratic air currents one has often to resort to his inclinometer and other instruments to keep right side up; for the fact that the water is level and of the same color when one looks ahead, has a disconcerting effect upon the vision. While flying over the clouds, which are generally of more level formation over the water than they are over land, the horizon is harder to judge, making aerial navigation very difficult at times. This has resulted in the use of several mechanical contrivances such as the artificial horizon, already installed on destroyers.

On a beautiful day in May I left for France —that is to say, it was a beautiful day in England. A little further south the weather was only half decent.

Providing the bus behaves well the trip from station to station can be made in an hour and ten minutes. That is rather a long time to be in the air without good landing underneath, and for that reason and the long delays and trouble caused by forced landings, we used to take a careful look at the weather before we left. On this occasion, a squall set in while I was half across the Channel, and I had great trouble keeping the pitching bus out of the water.

On another day I had picked a new route around the northern part of London. The

## BACK TO BLIGHTY

weather was fine and I had gone about sixty miles when the thought occurred to me that I would look up some of the boys at H., who were on home defense work. I had tea with them; then, at about five o'clock in the afternoon, I was ready to continue my trip to France. I said good-bye to the gang and got into my bus. From where I was I had to go due south and across the Thames River. I was not flying very high when on looking into the cockpit, I noticed that gasoline was spilling on the floor. I was unable to tell where the leak was, and rather than run chances I turned off my pressure. The motor stopped, and, as it did, I began to look around for a field in which I could land. I managed to get to earth all right, and then walked a mile to borrow a wrench, which I needed to replace the pipe that feeds the gasoline into the motor. Then I discovered that the tank was nearly empty. That meant that I would have to go in search of "juice."

I managed to get two gallons, and since I was consuming gas at the rate of eight gallons an hour, it was hardly enough to start with. But I had to get away soon, because a rain storm was coming up and I did not intend being caught in it in the open field.

I was at a loss what to do and so I consulted my maps as to the location of the nearest aerodrome. It was twenty miles away and in the direction of my flight. My two gallons of gasoline might take me there, and so I started off. About fifteen miles further on my engine again stopped, this time for want of fuel. Just then the rain storm struck me. I had taken the precaution to go up high enough so in case something should happen I would have room for a safe landing. But to dive in a rain storm is a very trying experience. The great speed of the machine causes the rain drops to strike hard, giving one the sensation that a thousand needles are being driven through the face. The water also blurs the sight as it dashes against the glass of the goggles, and the situation is rendered more difficult by the air currents, which during rains become very pronounced.

I had spotted the aerodrome I wanted to get to about half a mile ahead of me and started down for it; but I fell into so many

## BACK TO BLIGHTY

air holes and was bumped about so much by the currents that I began to fear the machine would be torn to pieces. I wished to land in the aerodrome, but feared that if I continued in the direction I was going I would end in a crash, as I had not enough height to make the 'drome. It seemed best to attempt landing in a field, and I was about to do so when some of the men from the aerodrome came out to help me.

As I tried to settle to the ground the men got ready to catch me by taking hold of the wings, which is the usual way of catching machines as they land in an aerodrome in strong gales or storms.

But for some reason that machine would not settle down but made straight for a fence. I tried to put a sort of brake on the bus by applying pressure on the tail skid. This is the only way one can stop a machine; the tail is light and the pressure is not heavy enough to pull a fast machine up in a short space, but it helped. Two men seized a plane each and my landing would have been a success had it not been that one of the men stubbed his toe and let go.

## THE FLYING FIGHTER

The part of the machine which was released began to spin about the part that the other man was holding. A tire flew off one of the wheels, and for a moment it looked as if I was to have a spill after all, but luck was again with me and I came out of it safely.

The aerodrome upon which I had landed was only in the course of construction, and for that reason I had to telephone to another aerodrome to get a tire, and the gasoline and oil I needed. Since there was no telephone at the 'drome, I had to go to a nearby village to attend to this matter. I had just started off when I heard a crash from the direction of the aerodrome. Looking around I saw an airplane standing on its nose. I rushed back to the aerodrome to see if I could be of any help to the poor devil, but found that he was dead. We had to cut his body out of the wreckage. Then we wrapped it up in a blanket. The poor man was an awful sight. His head had been completely crushed in. Right then and there I made up my mind that flying after all was a poor game. It occurred to me that any fool could fly, but that it took

## BACK TO BLIGHTY

a wise man to stay on the ground with both feet.

I rested up that night and on the next day flew that bus of mine to France and delivered it O. K. But all the time that I was up in the air I thought of my poor dead pal, for in the Flying Corps we are all pals.

The thought of quitting the flying business had come to me before, but there is a peculiar fascination about it. Hairbreadth escapes may momentarily sicken a man of the sport, but when the occasion has passed he longs to be up again in the blue.

The work I was doing had ceased to interest me. I wished myself back at the front, and made several attempts to get there. But the attack of gas poisoning had left my lungs in very poor condition, and constant exposure to the raw wind while flying did not seem to make them better. Still I wanted to be back in the game in France, or as Tommy calls the country, 'Ell. On the other hand, I had the consolation of knowing that so far I was not "pushing up daisies"—another expression of Tommy's when he wants to say that some pal of his has died. Meanwhile, I had made up my mind sometime to get a bus of my own and then fly to suit myself.

Testing and ferrying airplanes from one part of the world to the other had come to be my lot, it seemed. The air had now lost most of its thrills for me and the only surprise that came my way was when some comrade of old came to look me up.

One fine afternoon an orderly came to me with the information that there was somebody looking for me at the gate. To my surprise I found there one of the survivors of the old Tenth Canadian Battalion, and they were exceedingly rare now. The man's name was Maklin.

## CHAPTER XIX

### OLD TIMES AND NEW

Maklin and I had lived together in the same section of Canada, and he was one of those who had enlisted in the original three hundred that joined at Calgary. For a long time I had not heard of him and I had given him up for dead. The last news I had of him was that he had an eye shot out and had also lost part of his nose while rescuing his company commander from the barbed wire field in front of the trenches. For that Maklin had received the D. C. M.

When Maklin called he had with him Corporal Kerr, owner of a Victoria Cross. I took the two men into my quarters and there we got Kerr, after a great deal of urging, to tell how he earned the V. C.

"Well, you know," he started "we were out in the firing trench and we were doing our trick at sentry one morning at dawn. I was

## THE FLYING FIGHTER

just talking over with a pal how sick we were of trench life and how disgusted with everything in general. Just then a sniper from the other side picked off my pal.

"That made me so mad that I got over the top and started for the Hun line.

"I got over without being hit and rushed straight for the Hun trenches, hitting the bottom of one just at the entrance to a dugout.

"I hollered down to them to come up. The first two or three showed fight and I stuck them as they kept coming out.

"I kept sticking them until I had cleaned out that dugout. Then I went to another dugout, and as they came out I made them disarm and get over the top of their own trenches into No Man's Land.

"When I had the bunch out there I climbed after them and started for our trenches, just in time to meet some of the men who were coming over to help me.

"I had killed twenty Huns and had made sixty-two prisoners. Hence the decoration."

Kerr would not talk much about the other

## OLD TIMES AND NEW

stunts he had done, but he said that this one was nothing at all.

We passed a very pleasant afternoon together. Ham, my "side kick," took Maklin up for a ride while I showed Kerr the different machines. Then we talked trench warfare and finally drifted back to the experiences we had had back home.

While I was talking to Kerr a couple of Grahame-White machines passed overhead, and I explained to him that they were called Grahame-White bullets on account of the speed they did not have. These machines were then being used for training purposes.

To show Kerr what a really good machine could do, I got into a small scout flier of the DH5 type and went up. But my demonstration didn't work out. On taxiing out to get the wind, the under-carriage broke and let the bus down on one side. So I went back and resumed the "chin-chin" with Kerr and the others boys. That evening we dined together and talked of old times.

But life was still a matter of testing machines and delivering them. One day when the weather was thick I was scouting around

## THE FLYING FIGHTER

at about ten thousand feet. I noticed that the balloons were up all over the country, which meant that more weather was coming. The balloons in question are sent up by the London weather bureau in order that the general direction and nature of the wind and weather conditions may be learned.

When I saw the balloons I made up my mind that I would have to go still higher to escape the storm, but I had not climbed very much when of a sudden it grew dark and more sultry than ever. There was lots of clear blue beyond, of course, and I decided to make for that as fast as I could. I was doing very nicely when a black object loomed up in front of me. It was one of the weather bureau balloons. There was no telling what might happen in case I hit the thing, but to avoid it was possible only if I made a very sharp turn to the side. I twisted the machine around and missed the balloon by just a few feet. The current made by my propeller caught that gas bag, however. It began to swing wildly, and for a moment I feared that it might turn upside down. The men inside the car hung on to an armful of guy ropes for dear life. While it would have been impossible for me to help the men, I made a flight around the balloon. But the men in the car were now scared more than ever. They motioned to me to go away. I did not hear what they said but I guess it must have been quite unprintable. There was nothing else to do but to plunge into that haze again and continue going up.

At fourteen thousand feet I reached the top of that layer. I had started out in hot and sultry weather and for that reason did not have on my heavy clothing—just a dirty trench coat. The machine I was flying at that time used castor oil and a lot of it was always being thrown over the bus. It was cold at fourteen thousand feet, and I was just thinking of the many nicer places I could be in when the engine took a notion to stop. There was nothing to do but go down for the time being, so I plunged back into the haze and the cloud formation, and while the machine was planing down I did my best to find out what was wrong with the motor.

I was still within the sphere of the balloons, so between keeping my plane from going down on its tail, examining the motor, and keeping an eye open for possible balloons, I was kept rather busy. I was within one thousand feet of the ground, according to my instrument, and still the engine refused to budge. I began to look for a field in which I could land and discovered the pasture of a dairy farm. There was a large herd of cattle in the field but I had not noticed them on landing. When I saw them they were making for the fences and hedges in all directions with their tails up in the air. The trouble was that the said fences and hedges were all a little too high. Three or four of the animals were beached as they reached the top of the hedge and seemed to find it impossible to move either way.

The old farmer to whom the animals belonged did not appear to be pleased. He came out with a gun in his hands, and for a few minutes it looked as if he intended using that barker on me and the bus. The man was red in the face and mad clean through when he reached me.

"Ay myte! What do you think this is—a bloomin' 'eathenish picnic?" he shouted.

## OLD TIMES AND NEW

"What do you think I'm runnin' 'ere—a blinkin' circus!"

I explained to the wrathful farmer that I had not come down to scare his cattle on purpose, telling him that my engine had broken down and forced me to land in his field.

He wanted to know why I had to land in his field.

I explained to him that his field was the only one big enough to land in.

But that did not seem to improve the temper of the man any. He informed me that he was going to claim damages for three days' milk from the Government.

At first I did not know what he meant by three days' milk. Then he informed me that he was sure his cows would not give any milk for that many days.

From the looks of things I gathered that he was not far wrong. Some of the cows were still struggling to get over the fence one way or the other, and were having quite a lively time of it. But in the end they managed to get away.

A shot of brandy from the flask which I

always carry with me did not seem to make any appeal to the man. I offered him the flask but he turned me down. Then, in order to get the fellow into better humor, I offered to take him up for a ride, but he said that it was not for him. He had too much sense to go flying in a "bloomin' rattletrap like that."

Thinking that I might yet be able to do the man a favor I offered to take up his wife, but to my great surprise the farmer was madder than ever

We had a hard verbal set-to right then and there, and in the course of the argument I called the farmer a pro-German. This outraged him to such an extent that I really began to fear the man was going mad.

I decided to try a little strategy on him. I took out my notebook with a very serious mien and asked for his name and address. That helped. Of a sudden he grew very cordial and even invited me to come into the house for lunch. Being very hungry I accepted that invitation. After lunch I repaired my motor and then got the old fellow to hold down the tail of the bus while I started the engine. I had told him to let go of the tail when I motioned, and to take the sticks from under the wheels when I waved at him with my hand.

Everything progressed finely until the farmer went to take the sticks from under the wheels. He managed to get one of them away, and he was just starting for the other side when the machine started to turn, pushing the other stick out of the way. As the machine began to move the old man began to run.

Since I was in the wind I opened the throttle and started after the farmer, who was then going at a rate of at least twenty miles an hour and was gaining speed with every second. Just as I got up off the ground I took another look at the old fellow and found that he had caught his foot on something or other. He turned a somersault and then measured the remainder of his field to the fence by rolling all over himself. I turned back over the field and flew in a circle to see if he was hurt, but by the time I got over him he was on his feet again, shaking both fists at me. I made another flight over the field, wondering what made that man so mad, and then I noticed that something else was occupying the old farmer. The noise of the motor and the size of the huge bird had stampeded the cows again. Since I did not want to torment the old man any more than was necessary I made off for good, though I should have liked to hear what he had to say of me after that. There is no doubt that he wished I would break my neck or do something similar, but I finished my trip without further mishap.

A few days later I was to take another machine to the coast for delivery. Three other machines were in the group. We left about eleven o'clock in the morning, and we were near our destination when I saw a flock of Huns coming inland from the sea.

My machine had a gun, but I had no ammunition. We were near the aerodrome to which we were to take the machines and dove down to it with all possible speed to get ammunition. The other men had also seen the Huns and were coming after me with all possible speed. We had just landed in the aerodrome and were taxiing our machines to the shed, when a Hun bomb struck in a nearby field and exploded with a tremendous crash.

I had gone to see the commanding officer to get ammunition when an order came over the telephone that no machine destined for the troops in France should go up. That order had hardly been received when another crash came, and this time we took to our heels across the aerodrome. We were near the other side of the field when a third bomb crashed to the ground and exploded near us; so we ran back like mad. The Huns aloft seemed to have it in for us, and our running about merely showed them that their bombs were having some effect. Then somebody shouted:

"Lie down! Lie down!"

The order was accompanied by some caustic remarks, and we had hardly obeyed it when more bombs dropped around us.

By the time that the necessary ammunition had been issued to us and we were ready to take up the chase of the Huns they were well on their way home. This raiding party was never caught by the patrols in England, though those in France spotted them and gave battle, bringing down two of them.

On the following day we learned that a good many people had been killed in Folkestone, and that considerable damage had been done by the raiders. The result of our experience was the issuance of an order that in future all machines flying in England or being ferried to France were to carry ammunition. Most of the boys were praying for a chance to get even with the Huns. It was the first time that Hun flying machines had made a raid upon England and did any damage in that section.

## CHAPTER XX

### MEETING THE KING

Not so very long after that some of us got the chance we were looking for. Early one morning the alarm came that the German air raiders were coming. Those of us who had machines that were ready went up immediately, and others went up in machines that were not ready, the result of which was three rather serious accidents in which three men were badly smashed up.

But a few of us got up and cruised about at an elevation of sixteen thousand feet. In our hurry many of us had not taken the time to put on our heavy flying clothing, and these men came near freezing to death in that high altitude. We had cruised around for nearly an hour and a quarter when I saw one of our machines make a straight line for the sea. I followed, and before long I was able to count twenty-two Hun machines coming towards us. I recognized them as the big bombers used by the Germans.

The Huns were a little to one side of us, so that I and the other man who had flown towards the sea were on their flank. The man in the other bus was old Ham, as I learned presently. He had a faster machine than I had and was endeavoring to get above the Hun formation. After a while he succeeded, and then he dived through the Hun machines and separated them. After that the Huns proceeded in groups of four and five. Meanwhile I had overtaken one of these groups for the purpose of co-operating with Ham.

Within a minute or two Ham had spotted a Hun whom he seemed intent upon bringing down. I manœuvred into position, and when I thought the opportunity was good I took a burst at the enemy with my machine gun. The Hun started to drop immediately, and very soon I had lost sight of him.

Then I picked out another, and went to work on him. I was above him and took a dive during which I hoped to put him out of action with my gun. But as I plunged

## MEETING THE KING

towards the machine I found that I had run into a wasp's nest; I noticed that the air was full of blue streaks made by the explosive bullets which the Huns used.

I decided that I would have to climb again and try to take him unaware. I manœuvred upward and got a new position, but before I once more came within fairly good range of the Hun machine the men in it dropped all their bombs into the marshes along the coast.

It was necessary to act quickly if this machine was not to get away. The bombs had been dropped for the purpose of making the aeroplane lighter and enable it to rise more easily. The bombs had hardly exploded beneath us when the Hun machine started upward in a spiral. When I thought the machine was in proper position for me I dived under it and took it under fire from below. I had not spent many rounds of ammunition when I noticed the rear gunner in the Hun machine roll to one side; then he disappeared in the cockpit. At the same time the machine began to fall. But just then my gun jammed and before I succeeded in getting it to work again the Hun had managed to get such a start over me that pursuit was useless. I was given credit for helping to bring down one Hun by the commanding officer of the squadron, as some one else had fought him at a lower level.

But I had fared much better than a good many others. One poor little chap who had taken to the air in a "Sopwith pup" had gotten under the tail of one of the Hun machines. The man in the German machine got in his burst first and our poor chap got his in the head and started to spin earthward; I watched him until he was out of sight in the mist. Afterwards I learned that he had been killed.

But the Huns got their punishment before they left Allied territory, for the Naval gang patrolling the coast of France mixed in with them on their return home and brought three of them down.

The jamming of my gun had obliged me to quit the fight early. I made for the nearest aerodrome in the hope of getting another chance at the Huns before they escaped, but the all clear signal came before

## MEETING THE KING

I got off the ground. As the boys came in we heard very interesting accounts of the fight, but Ham was the only man who could be sure of his Hun. His observer, another man who was later killed, was slightly wounded. Ham's airplane had about twenty hits to my seven.

On the day following the big raid I was sent to the coast with a machine and returned early that afternoon. Another plane had to be taken to an aerodrome. I had gotten to the level of seven thousand feet, and everything was going along smoothly at a speed of about one hundred miles an hour, when all of a sudden the engine burst, and I thought for a moment I was hit by "Archie." The same instant castor oil flew all over me, and so completely covered my goggles that I could not see. As I felt about my face I noticed that something was hanging in front of me. The next thing I came to understand, after the first shock was over, was that the motor was no longer running. My feet had been forced off the rudder control. I groped around to find the stick but could not find it for a few seconds until I had gotten some of the oil out of my eyes. An examination of the various controls showed that the machine was totally unmanageable. I was falling—falling in such a manner that earth and sky seemed all mixed up. The machine passed from one loop into another, skidded sideways, then sailed on its tail for a second, righted itself again, and kept plunging earthward faster with every second. To my own surprise my presence of mind did not desert me. One moment I seemed to be sailing towards the sky, while the next left no doubt at all that I was rushing towards the ground.

Presently the machine began to swirl around its own axis while describing the regular spirals or spins.

I wondered how soon it would be over!

Another moment or two and then the crash would come.

I have never been much of a praying man, but then and there I said my little "Now I lay me down to sleep."

It was the only thing that came to my mind.

Then the thought occurred to me that I ought to make another effort to right that

## MEETING THE KING

machine, but in an instant I had discovered that it was useless.

Through my mind flashed every experience I had had, and I remembered how the boys had asked me what flowers I wanted for my funeral. I was just wondering what difference it could make to a man what flowers he might get when all of a sudden the machine righted itself and began to sail upon an even keel..

That fact restored me to normal. It flashed over my mind that I had just made a glorious nose dive, and I once more sought the control. But the stick would not move. As we say in the service, "It had taken the bone in its teeth," and that being the case there was nothing I could do to keep the machine righted. I was heading for the ground at the rate of about one hundred and twenty miles an hour, and, strange to say, had now given up all thought that I would be killed by the fall. I pictured the surgeons pulling struts out of my back and connecting rods from my knees. The thought filled me with a very peculiar fury. I would not go to another hospital if I could prevent it, no, not if I

## THE FLYING FIGHTER

had to break every control in the machine.

The machine was now diving towards some trees standing by a roadside. I feared that I would hit the first of them, but the machine just cleared them. Just as it "zoomed" over the top of the tree the displacement of air from the plane waved the tree-top, so close did it pass. I was not far from the ground now and still going at terrific speed. I would give those levers another try, I thought. I tugged away at them with all my might but not a one of them responded. The machine hit the ground and a hedge just as I was straining every muscle at the controls. The first contact threw me out of the cockpit. After describing three somersaults I landed on the ground, striking on my shoulders and neck. My escape had been truly miraculous, so much so that I began to feel myself all over in an effort to find the bones which I thought were surely broken. I felt no pain, and so with that I finally concluded that I was still whole. I lit a cigarette and then walked over to view the wreck of the machine.

I saw that it could be written off the lists.

## MEETING THE KING

I found that a defective tappet rod had caused the trouble, cutting the coul around the engine, which revolved at the rate of 1,300 revs. a minute, and that in some manner, which will never be explained, the propeller got tangled up with the machine gun and that the force of this contact strained every part of the machine to such an extent that it became unmanageable, allowing the engine to fall back on my knees and push my feet off the rudder control.

Some people came tearing down the road in a motor car. One of them was a doctor, who insisted that I should come over to his house for an examination. I had convinced myself that I was still in working order, but I wanted to reach the headquarters of my squadron by telephone, and for that reason I gladly accepted the invitation of the doctor.

When we arrived at the house I telephoned to the squadron and then gave myself into the hands of the doctor, who seemed to be a very painstaking man. But I will say for his wife that she had her husband skinned to death as a doctor. She went into the dining-room and presently returned with a bottle of Scotch whiskey, a glass, and some soda.

"I know what he needs more than anything right now," she said, as she poured me a drink.

And the lady certainly was right.

I am not a drinking man, but after a crash of that sort there is nothing on earth that will do a man so much good as a cigarette and a glass of Scotch and soda.

At about midnight a wrecking lorry and crew arrived, and by the first light of dawn we had the machine all loaded and on its way to the repair depot. The commander of my unit gave me five days' leave of absence for the purpose of having me regain my nerve.

The medico of the squadron told me that I had better go to a place where I would not see an airplane. To follow his advice, which I deemed kindly enough, I went to a little seaside town which has the reputation of being a very restful place. I had worn uniform so long now that I was anxious to find out how it felt to wear civilian clothing again. I bought myself a suit of flannels, and I did

## MEETING THE KING

enjoy the change from the eternal khaki very much.

The little place I went to is like most of the English coast towns—very pretty and picturesque. Some famous poet lived there once upon a time and every little landmark had its history. I stayed in a little inn known as the Red Cow, and one of the first things I did was to go for a swim. I had a good one. Then I went home and after dinner went to bed, because soldiers in England are so commonplace now that nobody looks at them any longer. I had a good sleep as a civilian, and next morning went out for a game of golf. I know little about that game, but the old man with whom I was playing was an expert. To make it interesting for me he gave me a handicap of seven holes. My partner also had a very fine line of golf stories and he could hit a ball so hard that it took two men to see it fly, one to say, "there she goes" and the other, "here she is."

We had just gotten to the seventh hole and I was doing finely when I heard a familiar hum in the air; on, looking up, I saw an airplane just about to land on the golf links.

## THE FLYING FIGHTER

Its pilot was a student and he had lost his way. He told me that this was his first solo trip with a war-type machine. I advised him to call up his squadron since he had landed in an awkward place. He was not so sure that he could get up again.

I took the man to the nearest telephone and as a reward the commanding officer asked me to fly the pupil home. I could not very well refuse, so I got into the machine and flew the pupil back to the squad. But the commanding officer was nice about it. He sent me back in one of the cars of the squadron, after we had lunched together.

Upon my return to the hotel I found a letter from the doctor telling me to be sure and keep away from airplanes. I wrote back to him that he would have to find another place for me, and that it would have to be entirely out of England so far as I could see. To keep away from airplanes in little England was quite impossible at that time. Two days later another landed in the sea just off shore and I had to help fish it out. When the five days' leave of absence were over I felt that I had had a change but not a rest.

## MEETING THE KING

I went back to the squadron and started to work again. A few days later we were told to put on our best uniforms. The King and Queen and Princess Mary were coming down to visit the squadron and we were to be presented to them. Four of us were to fly for the royal family and I was to be one of them. The machine I was to fly was one of the slowest machines, used for training purposes.

As the automobiles of the royal family and their suite appeared on the aerodrome, we went up. There was quite a gale blowing and it took some effort to get around the aerodrome. The machine I was flying was heavy and difficult to handle.

Near the aerodrome lies a railroad track and a freight train was coming down the line. It occurred to me that it might not be amiss to give the royal family a little exhibition, and with that in mind I started off on a race with the train. But the engineer brought off the honors. He left me behind, much to the amusement of the royal family.

On landing I was presented to the King, Queen, and Princess. To my great surprise the King recognized me again. That a man with all the cares he has should remember faces so well impressed me very much. The King asked me a few questions regarding flying, and in the course of the conversation I learned that he knew more about it than I had expected. The King is an honorary colonel of the Royal Flying Corps. He impressed me as a very able man, and I was glad that I had been in his service and had been given the chance to fight for a country like England. But for all that I never forgot the Stars and Stripes. I always carried an American flag in my baggage. One day a machine of a very advanced pattern was to be presented to General Smuts, the noted South African general. The machine was in our care, and our aerodrome and its buildings had been decorated in regular Fourth of July fashion. The flags of all the Allies floated over it except the Stars and Stripes. Ham and I inquired why this flag had been omitted, and were told that one large enough could not be found. We made up our minds to find an American flag that was large enough. It took two hours to do it, but by the

## MEETING THE KING

end of that time we had a flag ten feet long which we hoisted on the highest pole we could find on the hangars, much to the amusement of the commanding officer and the boys.

The presentation of the airplane to General Smuts developed into quite an event. The machine was given to the General by some Government officials, and then it was christened by one of the ladies present. Mr. Hucks, one of the old-time pilots, was instructed to fly the machine, and it behaved very well. Four of us did some stunt flying and amused the crowd for an hour or so.

A few days later an escort from our squadron was detailed to go to Hyde Park, where King George was to hold an open air investiture. About thirty men from various squadrons were detailed for the work, which consisted of patrolling at from 5,000 to 15,000 feet. To see the thousands of people crowding around the large stand that had been erected for the King was quite a sight.

Among those decorated by the King were a good many who had been crippled and maimed for life in the war. I felt great satisfaction in being able to assist at the ceremony, and to see men honored who had sacrificed so much in so good a cause.

A few days later I was sent to France with the last machine I delivered for the British Government. Five machines, in all, were to be taken over by this convoy. Mine was a two-seater, and I had a pupil with me whom I was to take as far as the coast, from which point I would be accompanied by an aerial gunner. The two of us were to fight off the Huns in case they should attack the flock. We met no Huns while crossing the Channel, but learned that they had raided England again on that very day.

Upon my landing at the squadron in France I learned that the Huns had done considerable damage to the aerodrome. One of their bombs had killed two equipment officers and a flight commander, who had been in the very act of going on leave of absence.

That night I went to B——, where I intended staying over night, having missed the afternoon cross-channel boat. There being nothing to do after dinner we decided to turn in, but had scarcely done that when we were routed out of bed by gun-fire. The Huns

## MEETING THE KING

were making another raid and were bombing the city. A couple of bombs fell into the camp of an ambulance unit and killed a few men. Another bomb killed a Chinese coolie and scared a hundred nearly to death. The Chinese were making off for the timber at an incredible speed when the Huns sailed away. It took some time to quiet that rabble.

After a while people came out of their cellars and resumed their occupations, but within two hours another Hun came over and started the ball rolling once more. The French "Archie" batteries were quite busy, and I was standing on the fire escape of the hotel watching the shrapnel explode, living over again meanwhile some of the experiences I have had at the front, when—zip!—crash! Just across the street from me in the fish market landed one of the Hun's bombs. It was a lucky thing that there was nobody in the market at the time or otherwise the list of casualties would have been long. After that the Hun disappeared and we were bothered no more that night.

There was little to do in our aerodrome now for a while. Now and then we would test a machine, but, the weather being very unfavorable just then and time hanging heavy upon our hands, many of us were given leave of absence. The same state of affairs prevailed at the other aerodromes, and a great deal of time was put in by the pilots visiting one another. It did us good to see again familiar faces, and most of the men had very interesting stories to tell. One of the friends who called on me at that time was Peter Gondie, who had joined the first unit to which I belonged in Canada. Peter had managed to get into the Royal Flying Corps, and one of his adventures was a fight with six Huns in which he had been hit by bullets four times in the knee. Peter and I had served together in the same unit for some time. He was a private then and I a staff sergeant. Like myself, he had since managed to get a commission, but was now about to be invalided out of the service.

Another man whom I met then was Capt. Foot, commonly known as "Feet," a famous British flyer, who has brought down many Huns. I met him in a theater. He was a very fine fellow. He had a peculiar habit of

## MEETING THE KING

flying without goggles and without a helmet. Shortly after I met him he went back to France and there added more glory to his name by mixing it with another gang of Huns.

I also met Carl Beattie in the course of this spell of inactivity. I had served with him in the ranks. He told me that he was waiting for some other friends of ours, and presently they showed up. One of them was Scottie Allen and the other Ballis. The former, poor chap, had lost his right arm. He had gotten into a fight with two Huns one day and had been hit seven times. The worst of it was that they had gotten him while he was still an observer; for that reason Scottie had never known what it was to fly a machine himself. We had all served together in a Canadian unit.

And we talked of the old times when we were in the Mechanical Transport Section in France and breaking our necks to get into the Royal Flying Corps. We laughed over our efforts to learn wireless telegraphy. We had made ourselves wireless keys and buzzers and had taken the batteries of the lorries to

## THE FLYING FIGHTER

furnish the necessary electricity. We had also managed to get a copy of the Morse code, as used in France, and after we had mastered the alphabet we used to amuse ourselves sending wireless dispatches to one another. That kind of thing has its value. When I joined the Flying Corps I was actually able to send fifteen words and receive about ten per minute. We also reminded one another of the days when we used to stop our lorries near an aerodrome on the main road to the lines. None of us ever passed that spot without stopping long enough to see some flyer go up or land. We thought of all the silly questions we had asked and of the funny replies that had been given us.

During this dull season somebody decided that we ought to take a course in aircraft construction at one of the largest plants in England. It was quite an interesting experience. Much of the work was done by women, to release men who were fit for military service in France. I was much surprised at the quality and quantity of the work done by the women. In addition to stretching the

## MEETING THE KING

fabric on the planes, they were helping in the building of frames, and they also put on the preparation which is used to shrink the fabric after it is sewed on. Some of them assisted in making propellers, while others varnished them.

The women of England have proven in fact that they can do anything that a man can do, and it is my opinion that if they were given a fair chance they would make just as good fighters. They are employed everywhere. Some of the ammunition works employ as many as 7,000 of them. They are nowadays also employed in France as motor drivers and clerks, and are quite capable of doing such heavy work as driving lorries. In machine shops I saw the women handle lathes and other machines. On the farms they do the plowing, and I doubt very much if England could continue the war without its woman labor. When we arrived at the factory there was a shortage in materials and for that reason we could not do very much, aside from looking over machines that were ready. Some of my time I devoted to the study of cloud formations and wind currents.

# CHAPTER XXI

### IN THE CLOUDS

THE problem of flying in clouds had always interested me greatly. There is no accurate instrument that will tell the flyer what course he is holding, and often this results in the man finding himself in dangerous positions while flying in thick weather. I have been in clouds so dense that I could not see the wing tips of my machine. Under such circumstances it is impossible for a man to establish what his position is in relation to the horizon. He is likely to come out of the clouds in almost any position. In fact, the squadron commander, who examined me as to my mechanical ability when I joined the service, once came out of a cloud on his back at a height of 6,000 or 7,000 feet, to find that he had dropped his observer out. He landed as fast as he could and started to search for the poor fellow, but the man

## IN THE CLOUDS

had been killed outright and half buried in the fall.

The oddest cloud formations may be met at times. Once I was up above the main stratum, which was about 3,000 feet thick, and was broken by holes here and there. I had climbed through one of these holes to the top of the cloud, but when finally I came clear the hole had closed up.

All I could see was a large white cloud that showed no breaks of any sort. There were large peaks on this cloud, and with my back towards the sun I started to fly towards one of them. As I came close to it, I saw on its very side the outlines of another airplane. I had seen no other flyers near me and I wondered where this one had come from so suddenly. Before long I noticed that the machine was coming towards me. I tried to avoid it, but found that the machine changed its position accordingly. I was sure that there would be a smash-up. I tried to get out of the way of the machine by a sharp turn, but that idiot of a pilot executed the same manœuvre. Then I climbed to get over him and the other machine did the same. A collision seemed inevitable. I closed my eyes and waited for the crash.

But I waited in vain. I had judged the distance between the two machines accurately, and after I was convinced that I had passed the other one I opened my eyes again—just as my plane was poking its nose into the cloud peak against whose sides its outlines had been cast by the sun.

As I rushed through the mist I was not yet sure that this had really been the case, so when I had emerged on the farther side I banked and described a circle around the peak to find the other machine. But there was no doubt that the machine I had seen had been the shadow of my own. I recalled then that the contour of the other machine had been framed in an iridescence showing all the colors of the rainbow. It occurred to me that it would be well to do it all over again, and I did. I reached the same position as before and went once more through the sensation of a crash in the air.

On another occasion I saw a peak that had a large archway in it. I made up my mind to fly through it. The peak seemed quite

## IN THE CLOUDS

close but I kept on flying without reaching the portal. What I had taken for a distance of only a few hundred yards proved ultimately to be ten miles. But I got to the archway in the end, and as I rushed through it the air currents made by the propeller caused the entire structure to collapse. In fact, I drew a great deal of it after me, the vapors following my machine like the tail of a kite.

Other peaks I tried to hurdle, but generally I would be deceived in the distance. I would imagine that I had gone over the peak only to find that this was not the case and I would find myself crashing through it. In other cases it would be still ahead of me, but once in a while I would come down to my former level close enough to the peak to dive through it.

Most of the pilots have a great deal of fun in the clouds, but they also find them very troublesome. Rain clouds are generally quite black underneath, and show all sorts of projections which are visible from the ground. Within the clouds themselves wind currents of varying velocity race back and forth. The bumps on the clouds are generally caused by the uneven density of the mists, and stand in direct relation to the wind currents beneath and within the clouds. The airplane going through a cloud of that sort may drop from two to three hundred feet at a time, without the pilot, who sees nothing but his machine and the vapor around him, noticing it. Clouds of that sort have been the cause of a good many bad spills.

I have often been asked by friends how one feels when up in the air some five miles. That is not so easy to explain, for on almost every trip a man experiences different emotions. It depends largely on the state of his nerves and on his general physical condition. But I may say that the feeling which oftenest came over me was that I had no business in those lofty regions. Not having lived the life of a saint, I could not help thinking of the hereafter and of the supernatural powers that are supposed to govern it; incidentally I felt convinced that there was a hereafter. At times it did not affect me at all.

But finally one comes to believe that his life

## IN THE CLOUDS

is entirely within the hands of the Supreme Power.

If that Power willed to put an end to my life on earth, it had but to fracture one of my planes or to demolish some other part of the machine. I would crash to earth then within a few minutes and certain death would be my lot.

There were times when, sailing up in the eternal blue with the noise of the motor the only sound to reach my ears—and even that becomes negligible after a while through constant hearing—I would experience a degree of lonesomeness that is impossible to clearly describe. Below me might pulsate a tremendous field of clouds, all gray and white, and around and above me nothing but the blue. On the earth it might be raining, but up there the sun was shining.

Under such circumstances one's life unrolled as though it were a supernatural moving picture. I used to review my past and find great satisfaction in the thought that I had never stolen anything nor killed a man in civil life. I took it for granted that if an angel should step out from a cloud and

## THE FLYING FIGHTER

tell me I had no right up there, he would know that much about me. But at the same time I resolved to obey his command immediately if he should order me to the earth.

Sometimes I would shut the engine off for the purpose of gliding down. I would then feel the absolute silence all the more, until the stays and wires of my machine began to sing and screech from the pressure while in a nose dive. With the wires strumming and the plane making the sound of a drum whenever the machine changed its position the veriest fraction of an inch, new thoughts came to me. They brought me back to the reality of things—the care of the machine. One never knew when a part of the contrivance, which had stood the strain of the last dive, might snap. In that case it would be all over.

Pilots and observers are a rather queer lot while on the ground. The language they use is not always of the best, and often they do things which are not exactly right, although as a whole they are of the best.

But up in the air it is different. In the course of time the flyer becomes very super-

## IN THE CLOUDS

stitious. He comes to believe in the queerest things. For instance, it is absolutely impossible to induce an aviator to be the third one to light his cigarette from the same match. Two or four will do so, but I've never known a man to have the courage to be the third. Some of them carry their superstition so far that they will not be the third man even if there are four.

They used to tell a little story of a squadron in France three of whose pilots were standing on the aerodrome one day waiting to go up on patrol. The three of them wanted to smoke, but had only one match between them. Two of them lighted their cigarettes on that match. It so happened that the third was a man who was not so very superstitious, or else he wanted to smoke very badly. He requested the privilege of lighting up. The others did not like that, for, according to the general belief, it is the third man who will be overtaken by disaster. In this case the man was very popular and his friends did not like to see him do it. But he insisted and they finally consented. He went up on patrol and while fighting off a Hun

## THE FLYING FIGHTER

was shot down behind the German lines.

That story was spread around, and thereafter the superstition was duly heeded throughout the Royal Flying Corps.

With many of the men, the mascot was really a fetish. Some of these fetishes were of a most peculiar character. The animals, which were kept in the camps, were looked upon as harbingers of good-luck for the organization. But each man had his own little fetish. It was known as the pocket-piece or mascot. In some cases it might be a dice or a playing-card. A man who had often drawn an ace to a full house, flush or a straight, was bound to look upon aces in the end as the thing that would bring him good luck. In other cases it might be a locket, then again a medal, while many of us carried little woollen dolls. Even photographs were said to have the quality which we expected of our fetishes. One of the men looked upon his pipe as a fetish, while another cherished a piece of Chinese jade upon which he counted. Another had a knife. Many of the men wore bracelets on one wrist. In fact, nine-tenths of the pilots in the Corps possessed some

## IN THE CLOUDS

queer sort of personal charm or fetish.

Some of the men carried these things only in their flying clothes, but others grew so superstitious that they would transfer them into a pocket of their other clothing; they refused to be without their pocket-piece at any time.

I remember walking down the Strand with a friend of mine one day. We came to a ladder upon which stood a window cleaner; inadvertently I walked under it. That friend called me every name he could think of for walking under the ladder. And yet he was the last person in whom I should have thought to discover any superstition. He was an old miner and a wild man besides. Later we returned to the aerodrome and I went up for a flight. I had tried my machine and looked it over carefully before leaving the ground. It was all right then.

Before going up my friend had warned me to be very careful, and I remember that in the act of gliding to earth I made up my mind to tell him that he was just a little too finicky about signs and omens. But on landing I broke my under-carriage and the machine was smashed up considerably before it came to a stop. I changed my mind after that, and carefully avoided walking under more ladders.

But that is not all. Some of us acquired the habit of finding omens in the queer contours of the clouds and the many fantastic shapes these mist formations will assume. Of course that was going rather far, but some of these flying boys become very superstitious.

The effect of nerve tension on a flyer who has lost his nerve may become permanent as far as flying is concerned. I have known men who would grow sick at the mere sight of a machine, and for this reason cease to be of any value whatsoever. Perhaps in the end they would come back to their job, and one would imagine that the man ought to be as good as ever. But that is not so. The thing that brings them back to the aerodrome is often a sense of duty. But the value of the man has departed; the flyer who loses his nerve once is lost.

It is my opinion that men so affected have brooded too long over the fact that in the

## IN THE CLOUDS

end the flyer is bound to be brought down.

There is a saying among flyers:

"If you stick to it long enough you're bound to get it."

And the saying is all too true as the casualty records show.

In the latter part of September, 1917, I had to go to a hospital, being afflicted with bronchial asthma. Everything possible was done to restore me, but I could feel that little good had come of the treatment I had been under. I was sent before a board of medical examiners, who recommended that I should be sent home.

I had been in Europe thirty-two months, and of this time I had spent twenty-two months in France, and the remainder in England, engaged in testing and ferrying work. And not a few weeks of that time had been spent in the hospital. Though I had been in the service for thirty-eight months, I was not tired of it, and if my health had permitted it I would have gladly continued.

Upon my arrival in Canada I was examined

again and found to be permanently disabled, having contracted chronic bronchial asthma, due to the climatic conditions of France and England, and the results of my old wounds. The board ruled that I was unfit for further service in His Majesty's armies.

While in the service I learned that a man never knows what he can do until he has to do it. I look upon my participation in the European War as the greatest honor that can be bestowed upon a man.

The army is one of the greatest teachers of all time. Its lessons may be costly, but they are of great value.

I cannot praise too highly the work done by the nurses and doctors in the Allied service in France and England, and to me they will always be the Army of Mercy. They are saviours of humanity.

# APPENDIX

## JUST FLYING MAN'S TALK

**AILERONS.** Movable section of the main planes located at the end and rear of the plane by which the bank for turning is obtained.

**A. M.** An air mechanic.

**ANEROID.** An instrument which registers approximate height and which is set before leaving the ground.

**ARCHIE.** Any Hun anti-aircraft battery, which sends up high explosive shells at inoffensive British or Allied birdmen, and which generally shoots too straight.

**ARMSTRONG HUT.** A hut about two-by-twice in size made of laths and canvas. The officers are expected to live in them. They are cold in winter and wet in summer and are named after the inventor, but they are about one per cent. better than a tent.

**ART. OBS.** Abbreviation for artillery observations.

# THE FLYING FIGHTER

**BELT.** A strap made of leather or canvas which the pilot wears around himself and which is fastened to the machine to prevent the pilot from falling when he comes out of clouds on his back or does some such other stunt.

**BUBBLE.** A curved spirit-level placed laterally to the machine, used to denote side slips but seldom used by experienced flyers.

**BUCKED.** Proud or pleased.

**BUMPS.** Air currents which upset the equilibrium of a machine by tossing it around. They make the pilot work when they are bad and they are sometimes dangerous.

**BUS.** Any flying machine or aeroplane.

**CANNBER.** The curvature on a plane. It is sometimes applied to a pilot's nose when damaged after crashing, or after a hot argument.

**C. C.** A mechanical device by which a machine gun is timed to the propeller to shoot through its blades while in motion.

**CHOCKS.** The only good things pertaining to flying. They are placed in front of the wheels of a plane when starting the engine to prevent the plane from running on the ground while testing or running up the engine, and they always stay on the ground.

**CHORD.** The width of wings.

**CONKED.** A new word which is taken from the Russian language and which means stopped or killed.

# APPENDIX

CROCK. Any soldier who is disabled for life through the European War.

DUD. A term characterizing anything bad or unfavorable, from weather to pilot and observer or gunner.

EGG BASKET. A tin box arrangement in which bombs are placed for strafing Hun balloons.

EGGS. Bombs weighing twenty pounds and upward filled with high explosives and "laid" in Hunland.

ELEVATOR. A movable plane fastened to the tail plane, by which the up and down movements of a machine are guided, providing the wires are not shot away by "Archie," in which case the machine comes down nose first and is wrecked. Some buses have a plane which is counterbalanced and takes the place of both tail plane and elevator.

FIN. A small plane placed on edge on the extreme rear of the fussalage, to which it is fastened. It is used to offset torque of a propeller or for added keel surface. The word is sometimes used in referring to each other's hands.

FLAMING ONIONS. A refined Hun device for bringing down Allied flyers when on low altitude night reconnaissance or bombing raids. They are about the size of a football, and, coming in contact with a plane, set it on fire.

FLIP. A flight.

## THE FLYING FIGHTER

**FLYING FISH HOOKS.** One better than the fire-ball and used by the same people. They are only on either end, to catch into the plane and make sure of burning it up if contact is made.

**FLYING O.** An O with a half wing attached to it showing the difference between a pilot and an observer. It is a brevet which can only be earned in France and is only worn by observers who have qualified.

**FORCED LANDING.** Landing through engine or other trouble.

**FUSSALAGE.** The body of a flying machine. When the birdman wants to tell a man he is going to hit him in the body, he will say: "I'm going to stave in your fussalage."

**GADGET.** The same as hickie.

**HANGAR.** A shed or structure made of wood, or a steel frame-work, covered with canvas, used for housing aeroplanes.

**HEINIE.** A German flyer.

**HICKIE.** This word is applicable to anything whose name you don't remember.

**HUN.** A student who is learning to fly, called that on account of the queer things he does. Every pilot is a Hun until he has received his wings.

**JOY STICK.** A contrivance by which a machine is partly controlled. So called because it adds speed to the machine when pushed forward, producing joy when the pilot is in a hurry to get away from "Archie."

# APPENDIX

**LOG BOOKS.** A set of books in which the record of the flying hours of an engine and machine are kept for reference.

**LONG RECON.** A trip of from 20 to 80 miles behind the Hun lines to gather information. Everybody goes sick when there is one to do, from which he returns if he's lucky.

**NOSE.** The extreme forward end of any flying machine.

**OBSERVER.** From pilot's point of view, human luggage ballast used to balance and help a machine while up in the air over the lines.

**THE OFFICE.** The pilot's cockpit.

**PADRE.** An army chaplain.

**PELOT.** The French term for pilot commonly used in the Flying Corps.

**PETERED.** Meaning to stop slowly or gradually.

**PETOT.** An instrument which records air speed.

**PILOT.** From observer's point of view, a chauffeur for the observer.

**POM POM.** A small anti-aircraft gun used from the ground on machines flying at a low altitude.

**PROP OR CLUB.** The propeller of a flying machine, generally fastened to the engine until displaced by high explosives. One or more are used, depending upon the type of machine.

**A PUP.**
**A DOLPHIN.**
**A CAMEL.**
**A HIPPO.**
Machines of the Sopwith make which bear some point of resemblance to the creature after which they are named.

# THE FLYING FIGHTER

**REV. COUNTER.** An instrument which counts the revolutions of an engine when it is running.

**RUDDER.** The only movable vertical plane on the machine. Fastened to the butt end of the fussalage and used in turning and correcting bumps.

**RUMPTY.** A machine of the Morris Farman type used in instructional work, called that on account of its queer movements in the air. It is sometimes called a longhorn on account of the long skids on the landing-gear and is a sister type to the shorthorn, which is minus this length of skids, and flies much faster.

**SAUSAGE.** A captive balloon which somewhat resembles a sausage in form. It is used by both sides for observation purposes.

**SCARFE MOUNTING.** A rotary mounting on which a machine gun is placed and used by a gunner or observer. It greatly facilitates the handling of a gun in the air.

**THE SKIPPER.** The Squadron Commander in the Royal Naval Air Service.

**SMOKE.** A name given to London, England, by Colonial troops on account of the heavy mist and smoke-like fogs which cloak it the greater part of the year. Usually "Big Smoke."

**SPAN.** The length of wings over all.

**SPINNING.** A stunt with a machine which consists of spinning the wings around the axis of the machine while diving nose first vertically.

# APPENDIX

**STUNTS.** Loops, spins or fancy turns made in the air.

**TAIL PLANE.** A section of plane fastened to the rear of the fussalage which it holds up.

**TAIL SKID.** A skid made of wood or steel tubing or spring-steel and which stops the tail of a machine from resting on the ground when not flying.

**TAKE OFF.** The getting off the ground of a machine.

**TAXI.** To run along the ground on one's own power.

**TENDER.** A sort of light motor truck used in the Royal Flying Corps.

**THOW.** A flying man's abbreviation for thousand.

**UNDERCARRIAGE.** The landing gear of a flying machine, same word being sometimes used by the birdman when referring to the pedal extremities of either sex.

**WAR HOUSE.** The place in England from where a great part of the war is run.

**WASSIN BIRD.** A French flying machine of the Voisin type.

**WIND UP.** A term meaning frightened.

**A WOLF.** A daredevil pilot who stunts near the ground. They generally last about a month.

**ZOOM.** A hurdle into the air—not to be practiced by beginners.